# Never Let Me Go

by Kazuo Ishiguro

D1338765

**Susan Elkin**

Series Editors:
**Sue Bennett and Dave Stockwin**

**HODDER EDUCATION**
AN HACHETTE UK COMPANY

The Publishers would like to thank the following for permission to reproduce copyright material.

**Photo credits**

**p. 10** david pearson/Alamy; **p. 20** AF archive/Alamy; **p. 25** TopFoto; **p. 29** AF archive/Alamy; **p. 36** Photos 12/Alamy; **p. 40** Artem Shadrin/Fotolia; **p. 42** AF archive/Alamy; **p. 56** Fotolia; **p. 67** david hughes/Fotolia

**Acknowledgements**

**p. 16** Guardian News & Media Ltd 2016; Telegraph Media Group Ltd 2016. Excerpts from *Never Let Me Go* reproduced by permission of Faber and Faber Ltd.

Every effort has been made to trace all copyright holders, but if any have been inadvertently overlooked, the Publishers will be pleased to make the necessary arrangements at the first opportunity.

Thanks to Dr Roger Pinnock for help with the medical science.

Although every effort has been made to ensure that website addresses are correct at time of going to press, Hodder Education cannot be held responsible for the content of any website mentioned in this book. It is sometimes possible to find a relocated web page by typing in the address of the home page for a website in the URL window of your browser.

Hachette UK's policy is to use papers that are natural, renewable and recyclable products and made from wood grown in sustainable forests. The logging and manufacturing processes are expected to conform to the environmental regulations of the country of origin.

Orders: please contact Bookpoint Ltd, 130 Park Drive, Milton Park, Abingdon, Oxon OX14 4SE. Telephone: (44) 01235 827720. Fax: (44) 01235 400454. Email education@bookpoint.co.uk Lines are open from 9 a.m. to 5 p.m., Monday to Saturday, with a 24-hour message answering service. You can also order through our website: www.hoddereducation.co.uk

ISBN: 978 1 4718 5364 7

© Susan Elkin, 2016

First published in 2016 by

Hodder Education,

An Hachette UK Company

Carmelite House

50 Victoria Embankment

London EC4Y 0DZ

www.hoddereducation.co.uk

Impression number        10  9  8  7  6  5  4

Year        2020  2019

Cover photo: © Pablo Hidalgo/123RF.com

Typeset by Integra Software Services Pvt. Ltd., Pondicherry, India

Printed in Dubai

A catalogue record for this title is available from the British Library.

# Contents

This guide is designed to help you raise your achievement in your examination response to *Never Let Me Go*. It is intended for you to use throughout your GCSE English literature course: it will help you when you are studying the novel for the first time and also during your revision.

The following features have been used throughout this guide to help you focus your understanding of the novel.

# Target your thinking

A list of **introductory questions**, labelled by Assessment Objective, is provided at the beginning of each chapter to give you a breakdown of the material covered. These questions target your thinking, in order to help you work more efficiently by focusing on the key messages.

## Build critical skills

These boxes offer an opportunity to consider some **more challenging questions**. They are designed to encourage deeper thinking, analysis and exploratory thought. Building and practising critical skills in this way will give you a real advantage in the examination.

## GRADE *FOCUS*

It is possible to know a novel well and yet still underachieve in the examination if you are unsure what the examiners are looking for. These boxes give a clear explanation of **how you may be assessed**, with an emphasis on the criteria for gaining a Grade 5 and a Grade 8.

## REVIEW YOUR LEARNING

At the end of each chapter you will find this section to **test your knowledge**: it provides a series of short, specific questions to ensure that you have understood and absorbed the key messages of the chapter. Answers to the 'Review your learning' questions are provided in the final section of the guide (p. 109).

## GRADE *BOOSTER*

Read and remember these pieces of helpful *grade-boosting advice*. They provide top tips from experienced teachers and examiners who can advise you on what to do, as well as what *not* to do, in order to maximise your chances of success in the examination.

### Key quotation

Key quotations are highlighted for you, so that if you wish you may use them as **supporting evidence** in your examination answers. Further quotations, grouped by characterisation, key moments and theme, can be found in the 'Top quotations' section on page 100 of the guide. All page references in this study guide are to the 2006 paperback edition of *Never Let Me Go* published by Faber and Faber (ISBN 978-0-571-25809-3).

*'Your lives are set out for you. You'll become adults, then before you're old, before you're even middle-aged, you'll start to donate your vital organs.'*
(p. 80)

## Studying the text

You may find it useful to dip into this guide in sections as and when you need them, rather than reading it from start to finish. For example, the section on 'Context' can be read before you read the novel itself, since it offers an explanation of the relevant historical, cultural and literary background to the text. In 'Context' you will find information about aspects of Ishiguro's life and the issues that influence his writing, and where the novel stands in terms of the literary tradition to which it belongs.

The relevant 'Plot and structure' sections in this guide may be helpful to you either before or after you read each chapter of *Never Let Me Go*. As well as a summary of events there is also commentary on the author's methods, so that you are aware of both the key events and the literary features in each part of the novel. The sections on 'Characterisation', 'Themes' and 'Language, style and analysis' will help develop your thinking further, in preparation for written responses on particular aspects of the text.

Many students also enjoy the experience of being able to bring something extra to their classroom lessons in order to be 'a step ahead of the game'. Alternatively, you may have missed a classroom session or feel that you need a clearer explanation. This guide can help you with this too.

An initial reading of the section on 'Assessment Objectives and skills' will enable you to make really effective notes in preparation for your written answers, because you will have a very clear understanding of what the examiners are looking for. The Assessment Objectives are what examination boards base their mark schemes on, and in this section they are broken down and clearly explained.

## Revising the text

Whether you study the novel in a block of time close to the exam or much earlier in your GCSE English literature course, you will need to revise thoroughly if you are to achieve the very best grade you can.

Reading this guide should, of course, never be a substitute for reading *Never Let Me Go* itself, but it can help. You should first remind yourself of what happens in the novel, and for this the chapter on 'Plot and structure' might be revisited in the first instance. You might then look at the 'Assessment Objectives and skills' section to ensure that you understand what the examiners are, in general, looking for.

'Tackling the exams' then gives you useful information on the exams and question format, depending on which examination board specification you are following, as well as advice on the examination format and practical considerations such as the time available for the question and the Assessment Objectives that apply to it. Advice is also supplied on how to approach the question and writing a quick plan, as well as on how to approach text in detail since some examination boards use an extract-based question for *Never Let Me Go*. Focused advice on how you might improve your grade follows, and you need to read this section carefully.

You will find examples of exam-style responses in the 'Sample essays' section, with an examiner's comments in the margins so that you can see clearly how to move towards a Grade 5, and how then to move from a Grade 5 to a Grade 8. When looking at the sample answers, bear in mind that the way they are assessed is similar (but not identical) across the boards. It is sensible to look online at the sample questions and materials from the particular board whose examination you are taking, and to try planning answers to as many questions as possible. You might also have fun inventing and answering additional questions, since you can be sure that the ones in the sample materials will not be the ones you see when you open the exam paper!

This guide should help you clarify your thinking about the novel, but it is not a substitute for your thoughtful reading and discussion of *Never Let Me Go*. The guide should also help you consolidate your approach to writing well under the pressure of the examination. The suggestions in the guide can help you develop habits of planning and writing answers that take the worry out of *how* you write, and so enable you to concentrate on *what* you write.

The guide is intended to complement the work you do with your teacher, not to replace it. At the end of the main sections there are 'Review your learning' questions to support your thinking. There are 'Build critical skills' and 'Grade booster' boxes at various points; these will help you develop the critical and analytical skills you need to achieve a higher grade. There is also a 'Top quotations' section, for characters, key moments and themes. Now that all GCSE literature examinations are 'closed book', this 'Top quotations' section will prove helpful in offering you the opportunity to learn short quotations to support points about characters, key moments and themes, as well as being a revision aid.

When writing about the novel, use this guide as a springboard to develop your own ideas. You should not read this guide in order to memorise chunks of it, ready to regurgitate in the exam. Examiners are not looking for set responses; identical answers are dull. They would like to see that you have used everything you have been taught – including by this guide – as a starting point for your own thinking. The examiners hope to reward you for perceptive thought, individual appreciation and varying interpretations. Try to show that you have engaged with the themes and ideas in the novel and that you have explored Ishiguro's methods with an awareness of the context in which he writes. Above all, don't be afraid to make it clear that you have enjoyed this part of your literature course.

# About the novel

*Never Let Me Go* was published in 2005. It is set in England in the 1990s, but it does not entirely depict that decade as it really was. Instead, Kazuo Ishiguro imagines that scientific developments have changed things since the end of World War II in 1945. It is, in part, a science fiction novel.

In Ishiguro's version of the 1990s, people with otherwise fatal diseases can be cured by organ transplants from living donors. This has created the necessity for a steady supply of people whose organs can be 'harvested'. After several organ removal operations, these 'donors' die. Such 'donors' are artificially created as clones (see p. 12 of this guide) and kept in institutions until they are old enough to have their organs taken.

Ishiguro, however, does not say any of this quickly or frankly. *Never Let Me Go* is like an iceberg. A tiny bit of what is happening shows on the surface. Most of the meaning lies beneath the surface. This means that the reader has to be very alert and must read between the lines. What is *not* said in this novel is often more important than what is stated openly.

The story is narrated by Kathy H., a clone who is due to begin donating her organs soon. Her story looks back in great detail at her time at Hailsham, the unusually idyllic school where she grew up. Its central focus is her relationship with two other students, Ruth and Tommy, who are both now dead.

The storytelling is quite convoluted, with many flashbacks as Kathy shifts backwards and forwards between her schooldays, the more recent past and the present. She drops tantalising snippets of information for the reader to pick up as she slowly unwinds her story.

Ishiguro wants the reader to think – and think hard – about some quite profound issues. For example what does it mean to be fully human? If a person can create art, enjoy music and books, have friendships and fall in love, then surely she or he is a human being with rights? Do the characters have anything at all to look forward to?

We ponder such questions with Kathy, Ruth and Tommy, as they cling to a pitiful hope that perhaps they can change their destiny if they can only prove their humanity. In the end they are forced to accept that their future has been decided for them by the authorities and that there is nothing they can do to alter it. This is a deeply pessimistic novel.

# Watching the film

*Never Let Me Go* was dramatised in 2010 as a film directed by Mark Romanek, with Carey Mulligan as Kathy, Keira Knightley as Ruth, and Andrew Garfield as Tommy. Although the film carefully depicts events from Kathy's point of view and uses flashback, it loses most of the subtlety of the novel. Ishiguro's novel rarely spells things out. The film is much more overt. It quite graphically shows a final donation and the death of the donor, for example. The film requires far less work and imagination from the viewer than the novel does of the reader.

Of course the plot is slightly different too. The film – which is only 99 minutes long – inevitably leaves out much of the detail, as well as the more minor incidents and characters.

In your GCSE you will, of course, be examined on the novel and not the film, so treat the film with caution. It is probably best to read the novel several times before you watch the film and then to do so critically, making sure you're aware of the differences and that you think carefully about the decisions the director has made.

If you watch the film too early in your studies there is a danger that you will confuse it with the novel, because visual images tend to be stronger in the memory than written ones. It may be best to consider the film as an imaginative response to the novel rather than as an interpretation of it.

Enjoy referring to the guide as you study the text, and good luck in your exam.

# Target your thinking

- What is Kazuo Ishiguro's background? (**AO3**)
- How does the novel relate to real-life medical research and ethics in the second half of the twentieth century? (**AO3**)
- How does the novel relate to literary tradition? (**AO3**)
- How have readers reacted to the novel? (**AO3**)

# The author

Kazuo Ishiguro was born in Nagasaki, Japan in 1954. His father, a scientist, moved the family to Britain in 1960 because he was offered a job in the UK. Ishiguro, then five years old, has lived in England ever since.

He did a degree in English and Philosophy at the University of Kent. Then came a master's degree through the University of East Anglia's respected creative writing course, from which he graduated in 1980.

Although Ishiguro's background is Japanese, he didn't go back to Japan to visit until 1989. He regards himself as a British author and it's certainly hard to see any Japanese influences in *Never Let Me Go*. He has said himself that he was brought up by Japanese parents in a Japanese-speaking home, and as such that part of his heritage has of course influenced his outlook, but probably not his major novels and other writings.

Ishiguro has written seven novels, including *The Remains of the Day*, which won the Man Booker Prize in 1989. *Never Let Me Go*, his sixth novel, was shortlisted for the same prize in 2005. He also writes short stories, screenplays (scripts) for films and song lyrics. He did not, however, write the screenplay for the film of *Never Let Me Go*; that was written by Alex Garland.

Kazuo Ishiguro was awarded an OBE for services to literature in 1995. In 2008 *The Times* newspaper included him in its list of the fifty greatest British writers since 1945.

In the summer of 2015, the University of Texas paid Kazuo Ishiguro $1 million (about £640,000) for a collection of unfinished manuscripts, drafts (including of *Never Let Me Go*) and scraps of scribbled notes. These now form part of the university's literary archive and are available for serious researchers to study. This is yet another indication of the worldwide status of Ishiguro as an important author.

▲ Kazuo Ishiguro

# Medical breakthroughs

*Never Let Me Go* mentions 'the great medical breakthroughs which followed one another rapidly' (p. 257) in the early 1950s after the end of World War II in 1945. Ishiguro doesn't specify what these breakthroughs were.

The novel, of course, is fiction and some of the medical breakthroughs have yet to occur in the real world. The first known successful blood transfusion took place in 1818. Gradually blood groups and the need to match patients to the right blood were better understood and, by the late 1940s, blood banks were established in many countries. Doctors have understood for centuries that, in theory, it ought to be possible to transplant an organ from a living or recently dead body into another person's body.

So what about the transplanting of organs such as the kidneys, liver, pancreas and heart? In the late 1940s a Russian scientist successfully transplanted a frog's heart into another frog. The world's first human heart transplant took place in South Africa in 1967. The patient lived only 18 days after the surgery, but his new heart beat normally until then. The first human heart transplant in the UK took place at Papworth Hospital in Cambridgeshire in 1979. Today, heart transplants take place every year and save the lives of many patients with diseased hearts.

In real life hearts for transplant come from people who have died in, for example, road accidents. Some people sign a donor agreement allowing their organs to be used if they die suddenly. In *Never Let Me Go* Ishiguro takes this idea a stage further, with the heart being taken from the donor when they are still alive, as the 'final donation' – something that in the real world is unthinkable.

It is possible, however, for one kidney to be taken from a living person, because the body can function healthily with just one. People sometimes volunteer to do this for a family member or even, usually through a charity, for an unknown patient. As with blood transfusions, there has to be a scientific match. There have also been sad cases of people in developing countries being persuaded to give a kidney in exchange for a relatively small sum of money, to save the life of someone in a developed country. The removal of a single kidney is probably what 'first donation' means in *Never Let Me Go*, although Ishiguro leaves such details to the reader's imagination. In real life there are, unfortunately, never enough donor organs and it is generally considered that too few people carry donor cards.

Ishiguro therefore is imagining a world in which such problems are 'solved'. If human beings can be created who aren't seen as fully human and whose feelings and rights can therefore be disregarded, then there will be an adequate source of living organs. These individuals are reared to adulthood and then subjected to a series of organ harvesting operations, until the fourth one – which kills them. This would mean that everyone else – in the outside world – could enjoy a life in which 'their own children, their spouses, their friends, did not die from cancer, motor neurone disease, heart disease', as Miss Emily puts it (p. 258).

**GRADE** *BOOSTER*

As you read *Never Let Me Go* make a list, with page numbers, of references to the physical sufferings of the donors. For example 'beneath the blotches', 'all hooked up', 'drugs, pain and exhaustion' (all on p. 5). These provide useful evidence to illustrate, for example, discussion about the presentation of fear of the future.

**Key** quotation

*'It was one of those little islands of lucidity donors sometimes get to in the midst of their ghastly battles.'*
(p. 232)

## Clones

Kathy, Ruth, Tommy, their Hailsham friends and the donors they later meet elsewhere are all clones – although the word is used only rarely, for example on page 256.

A cloned mammal is not the result of sexual reproduction. It is one that is grown artificially from the cells of another single individual and then transplanted into the uterus of a female surrogate who eventually gives birth to it. It is therefore genetically identical to the person whose cells are used, and does not inherit a mixture of characteristics from two parents. The process is very complicated but Ishiguro does not appear to be interested in the scientific detail.

The idea that Ruth was created identical to another human being, who could be living and working nearby, is the thought that drives the search for her 'possible' in Chapters 12, 13 and 14. Like any other human being Ruth is curious about her origins and background, but as a clone she has no parents so the 'possible' is the nearest equivalent.

**Key** quotation

*'Since each of us was copied at some point from a normal person, there must be, for each of us, somewhere out there, a model getting on with his or her life.'*
(p. 137)

In real life there have been many attempts to create clones. For example, a sheep called Dolly was created as a clone in 1996 and was regarded as a scientific landmark. At present it is not possible to clone primates because there are certain essential proteins that cannot (yet?) be created artificially.

During Ishiguro's lifetime reproductive technology has developed in many previously unimaginable directions. Eggs are now routinely fertilised in test tubes and transplanted into the mother or into a surrogate (this is in vitro fertilisation, or IVF). This process often uses donor eggs or donor sperm, or both. Ishiguro's idea of human clones is an imaginative piece of science fiction but it isn't, in the twenty-first century, particularly far-fetched.

Linked to this, there is no scientific reason why an artificially produced clone should not be fertile. It has all the same characteristics, including fertility, as the organism from which it was created. That includes the ability to produce fertile eggs or sperm and to be able to reproduce sexually. It is interesting, then, that Ishiguro chooses to make his clones infertile. They have sexual urges (p. 159) and enjoy sex but they cannot bear children (p. 82).

## Medical and scientific ethics

There are rules about what doctors and researchers may and may not do, based on what is considered in law – and generally – to be acceptable. Sometimes, though, the science develops more quickly than the rules. The science was very fast in *Never Let Me Go* too: 'there wasn't time to take stock, to ask the sensible questions,' says Miss Emily on page 257. 'Suddenly there were all these new possibilities laid before us, all these ways to cure so many previously incurable conditions.'

In real life it is now possible – using stem cells taken from a baby's umbilical cord after birth – to grow tissue that can be used to treat a sibling who has, for example, cancer. This means a couple could deliberately give birth to another child in order to save the life of an older one. You should consider how you feel about this. Recently it has become possible to create embryos, through a form of IVF, using genetic material from three people rather than two, thus eliminating certain disease-carrying genes. Many people, including doctors, are uneasy about this. Both these developments have come about since Ishiguro wrote *Never Let Me Go*.

Ishiguro barely discusses medical ethics in the novel, but they underpin the entire plot. At some point in the world of the novel, Ishiguro's fictional scientists worked out how to clone human beings and decided that their creations were subhuman. Apart from making sure they get proper anaesthetics, drugs and so on, they are treated merely as providers of organs.

Even the word 'donor' is strange and carefully chosen, because it normally implies a voluntary act of giving. Ishiguro's donors have no choice whatsoever. As so often in this novel, it's an issue that Ishiguro invites us to think about without openly spelling it out.

**Key quotation**

*'He was raising questions to which even the doctors had no certain answers.'*
(p. 274)

## The songs of Judy Bridgewater

At one of the Hailsham Sales, Ishiguro's narrator, Kathy, has bought a cassette tape called *Songs After Dark* by the fictional singer Judy Bridgewater. Kathy becomes extremely attached to it (p. 66), partly because she and the other children have few personal possessions; perhaps Ishiguro is also referencing the cultural importance of popular music to young people. She describes the cover and tells us it is a re-issue of an old 1956 LP recording.

The novelist encourages the reader to imagine how Bridgewater might have sounded to Kathy from her reaction to her favourite track, which contains the words 'Baby, baby, never let me go'.

Ishiguro has invented the song lyrics and then extracted the title of his novel from them – as a mildly witty response perhaps to many other novels with 'borrowed' titles, such as Thomas Hardy's *Far from the Madding Crowd* (which takes its title from an eighteenth-century poem, 'Elegy Written in a Country Churchyard' by Thomas Gray) or Agatha Christie's *Murder Most Foul* (whose title is a quotation from *Hamlet*). Using quotations for the titles of novels is a literary tradition.

**Key quotation**

'*...one or two other little episodes like that – started tugging at my mind.'*
(p. 41)

In Mark Romanek's 2010 film of *Never Let Me Go*, the Judy Bridgewater song is composed and used as theme music. It is important to remember, however, that in the novel the reader is given only fragments, upon which Ishiguro can hang incidents of importance to Kathy. These include the occasion when Madame sees Kathy listening to the words and hugging a cushion, the loss/theft of the tape, and the purchase by Tommy of a replacement for Kathy while they're in Norfolk.

## Literary tradition

*Never Let Me Go* is science fiction – a story that takes a scientific idea and extends or develops it for fictional purposes, often using the world it creates as a vehicle through which to ask philosophical questions.

The genre has a long history. Some people say that Johannes Kepler's *Somnium* (*The Dream*, 1634) is the earliest true example. It features an imaginary trip to the moon. Mary Shelley's *Frankenstein* (1818) tells the story of a scientist, Dr Frankenstein, who creates a human being – Frankenstein's monster – artificially. Dr Frankenstein's creation becomes a being with feelings (like the clones in *Never Let Me Go*), who eventually confronts his creator.

One of the best contemporary authors of speculative fiction is Margaret Atwood (born 1939), who is Canadian. Her 1985 novel *The Handmaid's Tale* imagines a world in which nearly all women are infertile, so the handful who retain their fertility become mere providers of an essential service (again, like the clones in *Never Let Me Go*) for the section of society that has power and that regards the 'handmaids' as a sub-species to be used for their purposes.

Like many science fiction writers, Ishiguro uses an imagined scientific outcome – a well-established live organ donation programme – and uses it to ask questions about bigger issues. His novel forces us to ask, for example, what characteristics make us fully human. He also makes observations about the human habit of refusing to face fundamental truths, such as the inevitability of death.

*Never Let Me Go*, like many other novels, is presented as a first person narrative. The story is told by one of its three main characters, looking back to her childhood and bringing the story up to the present. This is what, for example, Charlotte Bronte does in *Jane Eyre* (1848) and Charles Dickens in *David Copperfield* (1850). Twentieth and twenty-first century novelists who have told stories in a similar way include Harper Lee in *To Kill a Mockingbird* (1960) and Meera Syal in *Anita and Me* (1997).

The use of a narrator such as Kathy sets up an intimate relationship between narrator and reader. It is because we hear her voice that we never doubt that she is a human, enabling us to build empathy with her situation. On the other hand (see the 'Language, style and analysis' section of this guide, p. 62), Ishiguro makes it clear that we should not believe everything Kathy tells us.

The use of a character as narrator can sometimes limit the novelist's focus, because it makes it difficult to recount anything that happens in the narrator's absence. Novelists often have to resort to clumsy devices such as eavesdropping, repeated accounts, letters and other strategies. This isn't a problem in *Never Let Me Go* because Kathy's narrow range of vision suits Ishiguro's purposes very well. She is locked into only what she has seen and experienced and her own thoughts about them – and Ishiguro deliberately leaves the reader to infer what might be going on elsewhere. Her narrow vision is part of the way she is presented. She simply does not think much about anything outside her own world. It is her way of coping with the 'horror movie stuff' (p. 274).

### Build critical skills

Why does Ishiguro have his narrator reveal so little of the horror that making a series of involuntary donations actually involves? Make a list of references as you read of occasions when a veil seems to be drawn over the truth.

## Critical responses to the novel

When *Never Let Me Go* was first published in 2005, most critics found it a strange but compelling novel that was not really about what it seemed to be. They observed that genetic engineering and cloning were not its main point. 'Who on earth could be "for" the exploitation of human beings in this way?' asked M John Harrison, reasonably, in the *Guardian*.

Ishiguro 'simply uses a science fiction framework to throw light on ordinary human life, the human soul, human sexuality, love, creativity and childhood innocence,' concluded Andrew Barrow in *The Independent*. M John Harrison went on to say that the novel is really about 'the steady erosion of hope ... repressing what you know, which is that most people fail one another, grow old and fall to pieces.' Theo Tait, writing in *The Daily Telegraph*, regarded the novel as 'a parable about mortality' because 'we've all been told that we're all going to die but we've not really understood.'

## Build critical skills

Some have argued that *Never Let Me Go* is primarily a parable about death. With this in mind, consider that the fourth donation brings 'completion', but that some people complete unexpectedly at the first, second or third donation. Could this be read as a reference to real life, in which the exact manner of death is always uncertain and some people die prematurely?

Reviewers remarked upon Ishiguro's understated style and compared it with his earlier five novels, especially *The Remains of the Day* (1989). 'What Kathy doesn't know, we have to guess at,' wrote M John Harrison. 'His [Ishiguro's] narrators conspicuously avoid telling us the important things. Kathy H. is no exception,' observed Theo Tait.

Many critics commented too on the failure of the donors in *Never Let Me Go* to rebel in any way. 'Have they been brainwashed not to care?' asked Andrew Barrow. 'For the Hailsham students there are no efforts to argue and no redress,' commented Theo Tait.

## Build critical skills

To what extent could Ishiguro's clones have benefited from being more rebellious? When Mark Romanek's film version was released in 2010, Jenny MacCartney, film critic for *The Daily Telegraph*, commented similarly about the passive nature of Kathy, Ruth and Tommy: 'The plot suffers, as it did on the page, from how accepting these lambs are of their impending slaughter. A bit more attitude, some suggestion of rebelling against their lot, might have made its tragic inevitability all the sadder.'

People have continued to read the novel and debate its issues. As Theo Tait wrote back in 2005, 'The novel repays the effort in spades, building to a surprisingly moving climax and echoing around the brain for days afterwards.'

## GRADE *FOCUS*

**Grade 5**

To achieve Grade 5 you will need to show, where appropriate to the exam question, that you have a clear understanding of the context in which the novel was written.

**Grade 8**

To achieve this grade you will need to be able to make perceptive, critical comments about the ways that contextual factors affect the choices the writer makes.

## REVIEW YOUR LEARNING

(Answers are given on p. 109.)

1 When did the novel's 'great medical breakthroughs' occur?

2 Give three examples of diseases mentioned in the novel that 'the donation programme' has cured.

3 What is a clone?

4 What is the significance of Judy Bridgewater's music in the novel?

5 What indications are there that *Never Let Me Go* is widely accepted as an important novel?

6 What has the novel been discussed as a parable for?

7 Why, within the novel, have medical ethics failed to prevent the development of the 'donation programme'?

**GRADE BOOSTER**

For any good novel there is more than one valid interpretation. Candidates aiming at the highest GCSE grades are expected to show awareness of this in their answers.

# Target your thinking

- What are the main events of the novel? (**AO1**)
- How do these events unfold? (**AO1, AO2**)
- How does Ishiguro use structure in the telling of his tale? (**AO2**)

## Part One

### Chapter 1

- Kathy introduces herself
- The words 'carer', 'donor' and 'fourth donation' hint at the truth
- First mention of Hailsham
- Tommy's childhood behaviour at school

It is the late 1990s. Narrator Kathy H. is 31. She has been a 'carer' since she was 20, driving round the country looking after 'donors' who have been assigned to her. She is generally a good carer and therefore is sometimes allowed to choose her donors, such as Ruth, a friend from Hailsham. Hailsham apparently is an idyllic and rather elitist boarding school, envied by people who were at different schools. Ishiguro gives us a first glimpse into what it means to be a donor with the words 'all hooked up' and 'drugs, pain and exhaustion' (p. 5). Kathy also mentions the sinister-sounding 'fourth donation' (p. 1). Kathy will finish her carer's job in the next few months. Reminiscing about her childhood at Hailsham, Kathy thinks about another school friend, Tommy, who was bullied for his frequent, flamboyant tantrums. She recalls a day when she tried to help him and he accidentally hit her. Later, as an adult carer, she became close again to both Ruth and Tommy when they became donors.

**Key quotation**

'...*as he threw up his arm, he knocked my hand aside and hit the side of my face.*'
(p. 11)

### Chapter 2

- An apology
- Tommy's childish art
- Exchanges of treasured artwork by students
- Tommy relentlessly bullied
- Something changes Tommy at about 13

Reminiscing about her childhood at Hailsham, Kathy remembers that Tommy apologised to her for hitting her, which makes her think further about his behaviour. She tries, unsuccessfully, to stop the bullying by speaking to the other girls. 'Exchanges' are quarterly school events, in which pupils 'sell' their art and other small items to each other for tokens. Kathy remembers these occasions when she is Ruth's carer many years later. Tommy's art is immature – although art lessons given by Miss Geraldine and others are very important at Hailsham – and he contributes nothing to the exchanges, which is partly why he gets bullied in games and other lessons. Other boys and girls also enjoy his dramatic reactions. Persecution of Tommy and his associated tantrums stop when he is about thirteen. Privately he promises to explain to Kathy what has happened to change him.

## Chapter 3

- Miss Lucy tells Tommy that art does not matter
- First mention of Madame's Gallery
- Ruth demonstrates that Madame is frightened of her and her friends
- Early awareness that Hailsham children are 'different'

Tommy tells Kathy that Miss Lucy, one of the Hailsham guardians, has told him that not being creatively talented doesn't matter. Kathy is very surprised because creativity is central to the Hailsham approach to education. Tommy had noticed that Miss Lucy seemed to be angry and had concluded that her attitude was something to do with the children's futures as donors. The woman they call Madame visits the school regularly and takes away the best of the children's art for her presumed Gallery. Madame's 'Gallery' is a very well established school rumour although it is in a 'hazy realm'. Ruth believes Madame is frightened of the Hailsham students and organises the others to crowd in on Madame when she arrives. Madame looks scared, so they conclude that Ruth is right. With hindsight, Kathy concludes that even when very young she and the other Hailsham students were always, at some level, aware that they were different from others.

### Key quotation

*Kathy describing Madame's Gallery, but could also be applied to the very vague awareness of young Hailsham students of their future: 'hazy realm'.*
(p. 32)

## Chapter 4

- The 'tokens controversy'
- Miss Emily's assemblies
- Infant Kathy first plays with Ruth

Kathy remembers developments when she and the others were about ten. Part of the Hailsham culture was the amassing of 'collections' of other students' art. Some students feel that if Madame takes away their best work they would earn fewer tokens with which to buy items from others. Tokens are also used to buy things from Sales, when boxes of bits and pieces are brought in from outside. The fairness – or not – of the tokens system is openly discussed in Miss Lucy's lesson when students bring it up. Kathy recalls Miss Emily's sometimes puzzling daily assemblies and thinks back to first getting friendly with Ruth when they were in the infants.

▲ Ruth and Kathy as schoolgirls in the 2010 film adaptation

## Chapter 5

- Secret guard for Miss Geraldine
- Ruth's pencil case

Ruth starts a little gang of friends to defend Miss Geraldine, their favourite guardian, from plots that they believe, or pretend, exist against her. It turns into a power base for Ruth, although Kathy is disappointed to realise that Ruth has lied about being able to play chess. Gradually the children outgrow the 'secret guard' and it fades away. Later Ruth acquires a special pencil case, envied by the others, and implies it is a gift from Miss Geraldine, although that would have been strictly 'beyond the bounds'. Kathy seriously upsets Ruth – which she deeply regrets – by pretending that she has consulted the Sales register and caught Ruth out in a lie about the pencil case.

# Chapter 6

- The pencil case issue continues
- Kathy tries to be supportive to Ruth
- Madame sees Kathy dancing in the dormitory
- Kathy's tape is stolen
- Ruth gives her another tape

In 'remorse and frustration', Kathy tries to make things right with Ruth by behaving as if the latter really does have a special relationship with Miss Geraldine. Meanwhile, another child notices that Ruth is no longer using the pencil case, and Kathy pretends that she knows where it came from. Then Kathy's favourite tape, *Songs After Dark* by Judy Bridgewater, bought in a Sale, disappears from her collection. Perhaps it has gone to Norfolk, where the children believe lost property is stored? Kathy thinks back to an earlier occasion when she was listening alone in her dormitory to the track 'Never let me go'. Holding a pillow and pretending it was a baby, she was dancing with her eyes closed when Madame passed the open door. Madame wept and Kathy didn't understand why – unless it was revulsion. The tape has now completely disappeared and the implication, not spelled out, is that Ruth has destroyed it. Later, she presents Kathy with a different tape as a compensatory gift.

## Key quotation

'*...what I was doing was swaying about slowly in time to the song, holding an imaginary baby to my breast.*'
(p. 71)

> **Build critical skills**
>
> Make notes on all the possible implications of the title *Never Let Me Go* within the text of the novel. How appropriate do you think the title is, and why?

# Chapter 7

- The final years at Hailsham
- Miss Lucy tells them the truth
- Sex education
- Tommy's injured arm

Kathy describes the last three years at Hailsham, from age 13 to 16, and remembers troubled Miss Lucy, who was different from the other guardians in apparently wanting to give the students more information about their futures. One day she spells it out bluntly. They will serve as carers and then will themselves become donors of their vital organs. There is no other future. Meanwhile, all the students are given frank sex education lessons and encouraged to experiment for pleasure (they are physically unable to conceive children). Tommy's arm injury and his fears about it show just how little they still understand about donations and their bodies.

## Key quotation

'*What she was talking about was, you know, about us. What's going to happen to us one day. Donations and all that.*'
(p. 29)

**Build critical skills**

The students, according to Miss Lucy and Kathy (with hindsight), agree they have been 'told and not told' about the life that lies ahead of them. No one has lied to them exactly, but they have been protected from understanding fully until Miss Lucy spells it out. Is it at all justified that the truth is withheld from the children at Hailsham? Make notes on your views.

## Chapter 8

- Kathy observes Miss Lucy apparently angry
- Tommy's old problems resurface
- Students, including Ruth and Tommy, begin having sex
- Kathy plans sex with Harry C.

Miss Lucy is alone in a quiet part of Hailsham and Kathy, now 16, sees her angrily crossing something out in a document. Tommy's mood has changed and he is being bullied and getting into rages again. Kathy presumes that this is connected to his old problems about his lack of creativity and to his break-up with Ruth, with whom he'd been in a relationship for six months. Many students now seem to be having sex – although some of it may be just talk – and Kathy decides she will have it with Harry C. but, despite earnest preparations, she keeps putting it off.

## Chapter 9

- Kathy thinks about becoming Tommy's partner
- Miss Lucy tells Tommy that art is 'evidence'
- Miss Lucy leaves the school
- Ruth and Tommy resume life as a couple

Kathy considers starting a sexual relationship with Tommy as Ruth's 'natural successor' (p. 98) following their break-up, and remembers years later meeting Harry – with whom she did not in the end have sex – in a recovery centre after a donation. Back at Hailsham, Ruth asks Kathy to help her to get back with Tommy. Although she is surprised and a bit disappointed, she agrees to talk to him. When she does, Tommy tells her that Miss Lucy has told him that she made a mistake (see Chapter 3, above) and that being creative *is* important for Hailsham students after all. Art is 'evidence' of something, which neither Tommy nor Kathy understands. Not long after that, Miss Lucy suddenly leaves Hailsham. Although Tommy is doubtful when he speaks to Kathy about resuming his relationship with Ruth, he is soon back with her.

**Key quotation**

*Ruth reporting Tommy's comments about Kathy: 'How you've got guts and how you always do what you say you're going to do. He told me once that if he was in a corner he'd rather you were backing him than any of the boys'*
(p. 102)

# Part Two

## Chapter 10

- Kathy, Ruth and Tommy arrive at the Cottages
- Ruth and Tommy continue as a couple
- Kathy finds Ruth's showing off puzzling and annoying

Kathy remembers arriving at the Cottages, one of a number of communities across the country where former students from Hailsham and other schools live in independent isolation for a period between leaving school and beginning their carer training. Kathy, Ruth and Tommy are all sent to the Cottages, where they are allowed – in the company of others, some of them a little older – to live an 'easy going' and 'languid' existence with few demands made on them. Ruth and Tommy are accepted by the others as a couple and Kathy is irritated by the silly habits Ruth picks up from other couples, such as punching Tommy's arm as a greeting. Everyone reads books and most, especially Ruth, pretend to know more about life than they do. Kathy sleeps, quite casually, with a couple of the young men at the Cottages but doesn't regard it as significant.

**Key quotation**

*'...fearful of the world around us, and – no matter how much we despised ourselves for it – unable quite to let each other go.'*
(p. 118)

## Chapter 11

- 'Functional' sex at the Cottages
- Kathy worries about sexual desire
- Kathy scans pornographic magazines for faces

In the more adult atmosphere of the Cottages, residents can have casual sex if they wish and Kathy does, while Ruth remains in a relationship with Tommy. Although Ruth can be gratingly unpleasant, she and Kathy remain friends over bedtime drinks. Meanwhile, Kathy experiences raw sexual desire and wonders whether that's normal. Tommy finds her systematically flicking through pornographic magazines. She isn't looking for titillation, however; she's studying the faces of the models, although she pretends that it's 'for kicks' and doesn't tell Tommy what she is really searching for until months later.

**Key quotation**

*'I checked each model's face before moving on.'*
(p. 132)

## Chapter 12

- Chrissie and Rodney have seen someone who might be Ruth's 'possible'
- Norfolk trip planned

Every clone has been created from a natural human being, who must be around somewhere in the 'Real World'. Chrissie and Rodney, slightly in awe of Ruth, Tommy and Kathy's Hailsham status, claim to have spotted a 'possible' for Ruth working in an office in Norfolk. Ruth is very excited about this, especially as her fantasy 'dream future' is to work in a shiny modern office. The five of them – Chrissie, Rodney, Ruth, Tommy and Kathy – plan a trip to Norfolk.

## Chapter 13

- Rodney borrows and drives a car
- Journey to Norfolk
- Chrissie tentatively asks about deferrals
- Ruth and Tommy are both upset

The five of them travel to Norfolk in a car borrowed and driven by Rodney. Ruth behaves awkwardly during the journey and seems to be showing off to the veterans. On arrival in a Norfolk coastal town they go to a café – a very novel experience – where Chrissie raises the subject of deferrals. She has heard rumours that, if you can convince the authorities that you're genuinely in love, you can postpone your fate as a carer and then donor. She thinks the Hailsham students will know the details and Kathy realises that this is the real reason for the Norfolk trip. Ruth and Tommy both become very upset – in different ways – because the truth is that none of them knows anything solid about deferrals, but all of them hope it's true – against everything they've ever been told.

## Chapter 14

- Shopping in Woolworths
- Kathy overhears Chrissie quizzing Ruth further about deferrals
- All five pass by the office where Ruth's 'possible' works and follow her to an art gallery
- Ruth realises that the woman is nothing to do with her and becomes very bitter
- Chrissie, Rodney and Ruth leave Kathy and Tommy alone

The five students shop in Woolworths so that Chrissie can buy some greetings cards and, when she thinks no one is listening, can question Ruth further in search of privileged information she thinks the Hailsham students might have about deferrals. They then walk to the office where Chrissie and Rodney have seen Ruth's possible. After watching the woman through the window they follow her (when she, by chance, emerges) to a small art gallery/shop. They soon realise that the woman is nothing like Ruth; this triggers a common-sense observation from Kathy that there is no likelihood of students having similar lifestyles and expectations to their clone originators, which results in an embittered outburst from Ruth. With tension in the air, Chrissie and Rodney take Ruth to visit a carer friend, Martin, leaving Kathy and Tommy together.

▲ Rodney, Kathy, Ruth and Chrissie in the 2010 film

# Chapter 15

- Kathy learns that Tommy wants to buy her a replacement tape
- They find the tape and cheer up
- Tommy shares his theory about the Gallery
- He is now doing artwork to try and save himself
- Kathy reveals her strong – and confusing – sexual urges

Tommy wants to find a present for Kathy – a Judy Bridgewater tape to replace the one with the 'Never let me go' track that disappeared at

Hailsham. Kathy finds the tape in a box in a backstreet second-hand shop and Tommy buys it for her. Even years later the two of them remember how happy this makes them. On leaving the shop Tommy seems downcast again and tells Kathy that he has concluded that the purpose of Madame's Gallery was to reveal students' souls for deferral decisions – in which case he is doomed because he contributed nothing to the Gallery. He is now trying to amass a portfolio of highly stylised tiny animal drawings to compensate. Kathy discusses with Tommy her random stabs of indiscriminate sexual desire and he tries to reassure her that this is normal. A tacit decision is made that none of this is to be discussed with Ruth.

## Chapter 16

- Kathy sees Tommy's drawings in the Goosehouse
- Ruth irritates Kathy by pretending to forget things that happened at Hailsham
- Ruth and Kathy laugh together about Lenny and Tommy
- Ruth sneers at Tommy's drawings and theory

Kathy comes across Tommy in one of the barns at the Cottages that he is using as a secret studio. She is drawn to his intricate, vulnerable, metallic animals. Meanwhile, Ruth annoys her by refusing to remember some very memorable things about Hailsham. But the relationship with Ruth is changeable and, girls together, they laugh about Lenny, a veteran now gone to start his training, with whom Kathy has been having sex, and about Tommy's drawings. Ruth is startled to find the Judy Bridgewater tape among Kathy's possessions. On a walk to a nearby old country church, Kathy finds Ruth and Tommy. Ruth is calculatedly dismissive of Tommy's art and its purpose, which makes Kathy feel uncomfortable.

## Chapter 17

- Kathy finds it harder to talk to Tommy
- Ruth argues that Tommy could never fancy Kathy sexually
- Kathy decides to leave the Cottages and begin her training

As their second year at the Cottages passes, Kathy realises that the aftermath of the incident at the church is that she now finds talking to Tommy awkward. When she tries to put things right by talking frankly to Ruth, the latter tells her that – even if he were no longer in a relationship – Tommy would not want to be a couple with Kathy because she has had casual sex with others. Not long after that, Kathy volunteers to begin her training as a carer and soon it is time for her to leave the Cottages and the people who live there.

Why, in your view, does Ishiguro have Kathy take the decision to leave the Cottages to begin training when she doesn't yet have to? It means that she doesn't see either Ruth or Tommy again for nearly ten years.

**Key quotation**

*'It wasn't long after that I made my decision, and once I'd made it, I never wavered.'*
(p. 199)

# Part Three

## Chapter 18

- Kathy works as a carer and learns the skills
- She talks to another carer, Laura, a former Hailsham student
- She becomes Ruth's carer at Dover
- Plans to visit Tommy gradually firm up

Kathy now drives around the country from recovery centre to centre supporting 'her' assigned donors, some of whom don't do well even at first donation. This, she learns from distressed and exhausted fellow ex-Hailsham carer Laura and from rumours from elsewhere, is what has happened to Ruth. Kathy, as an experienced and respected carer, now has some choice over 'her' donors so she becomes Ruth's carer at Dover. They discuss old times at length, although the things that really need to be talked about are carefully and awkwardly avoided. Ruth tells her she wants a trip to visit a beached boat, but really she wants to see Tommy, whose recovery centre is nearby. Eventually Kathy agrees to this.

**Key quotation**

Kathy about Dover: *'... and I wouldn't mind at all if that's where I ended up.'*
(p. 17)

## Chapter 19

- Kingsfield, where Tommy is based
- Kathy drives Ruth, now frail, and Tommy to the boat
- They talk about friends who have completed too soon
- Ruth admits that Tommy and Kathy should be a couple
- She urges them to go for a deferral
- Ruth dies at second donation

Kathy takes Ruth to Kingsfield, a former holiday camp that is now a recovery centre, where Tommy is based after his second donation. He seems physically stronger than Ruth, who is evidently quite ill after hers. After a fairly strained car journey they visit and admire the boat, although Ruth finds the walk and bending quite difficult.

Talk turns to the fate of Chrissie, who is now dead, and Rodney, who is apparently 'doing okay', and to Ruth's repeated belief that people probably often die at second donation. Donors, she argues, are not told this. On the journey back, Ruth eventually voices something she's been thinking about

**Key quotation**

*'Tommy seemed to become aware for the first time just how frail she was.'*
(p. 218)

Key quotation

**Key** quotation

*'You and Tommy, you've got to try and get a deferral.'*
(p. 228)

for a long time. She thinks that Tommy and Kathy should get together as a couple, saying she deliberately kept them apart and asking for their forgiveness. Ruth urges them to try and get a deferral and presents Tommy with Madame's address, which she has gone to a lot of trouble to get. At the end of the chapter we see Kathy sitting with Ruth for the last few hours of her life after the latter's second – and final – donation.

### Build critical skills

What can you deduce about the complicated friendship between Ruth and Kathy from the language Ishiguro gives them to speak in the conversation on pages 196–98? Try speaking it as if it were a play, implying the undercurrents of feeling between the two characters.

## Chapter 20

- Kathy becomes Tommy's carer after his third donation
- They become comfortable together and begin a sexual relationship
- They agree to visit Madame with Tommy's drawings

A year after the trip to see the boat Kathy becomes Tommy's carer and spends as much time as she can with him at Kingsfield, relaxing, reminiscing and, eventually, having sex. In time they begin to discuss the deferral issue, as Tommy has now come through his third donation and notice of his fourth could arrive soon. They plan a visit to Madame's house in Littlehampton, a seaside resort in Sussex, taking Tommy's drawings with them. Kathy has quietly been there on her own already and watched Madame arriving home so they are certain of her whereabouts.

## Chapter 21

- Very nervously, Kathy and Tommy call at Madame's house
- They tell Madame why they've come
- Tommy explains what he believes to have been the purpose of Madame's Gallery
- Miss Emily emerges from where she's been eavesdropping

Kathy and Tommy are very apprehensive and tense on arrival in Littlehampton. Eventually they see Madame returning home, speak to her on her front path and are invited in. Together they explain the purpose of their visit and Tommy tells her his theory that the collected art was to use as evidence of students' souls in deferral application cases. Madame seems both puzzled and distressed. Miss Emily, now a wheelchair user, then emerges from a dark part of the room in this dingy old house, which is full of art and photographs, including one of Hailsham. She has been listening in to the conversation and her entrance is quite dramatic.

▲ Kathy and Tommy in the 2010 film

## Chapter 22

- Miss Emily explains the thinking behind Hailsham and how it failed in the end
- She and Madame gently sympathise with the students
- Kathy and Tommy are told firmly that there are no deferrals ever, not for anyone
- Tommy loses control of his emotions in a field on the way back to Kingsfield

Miss Emily and Madame (whose name is Marie-Claude) have been working together for a long time and now share a home. Their life's work, Miss Emily explains, was to set up an ideal environment – Hailsham – and to give the clones in their charge, known as 'students', a childhood as normal as possible, with education, art and contentment.

They did this out of a belief that even clones have souls that should be nurtured; Hailsham, very unlike many other institutions, was an attempt to demonstrate this to the authorities. Ultimately they failed. Hailsham closed after the 'Morningdale scandal', which turned the tide of public opinion. Miss Emily and Madame lost a substantial amount of money over Hailsham and even now are having to sell possessions (a bedside cabinet today) to make ends meet. Everything that faces the students is bleak; there are no deferrals. 'Your life must now run the course that's been set for it,' says Miss Emily (p. 261). After Miss Emily goes off by car with her carer, George, Kathy reminds Madame of the 'Never let me go' track on her tape and Madame explains what moved her when she saw Kathy dancing (see Chapter 6). Kathy and Tommy drive back to Kingsfield. On the way, Tommy gets out of the car and has one of his old tantrums of despair.

**Key** quotation

*'They don't tell you the half of it, you see?'*
(p. 222)

**GRADE** *BOOSTER*

Remember, you need to know the plot really well. It is also important to bear in mind, however, that you will never be set an examination question that requires you simply to recount the plot. Always use your knowledge of the plot to shape your answer to the question asked.

# Chapter 23

- Tommy begins to separate himself from Kathy
- Notice comes for his fourth donation
- He tells her he'd rather she weren't his carer through the last stage of his life
- Kathy reflects on her losses

Once he realises that there is no future for him with Kathy, Tommy begins to put distance between them. They don't talk so freely and he tells her not to organise his laundry. When the notice comes for his fourth donation, he tells Kathy that he doesn't want her to be his carer 'through this last bit'. A few quiet weeks follow, which include Tommy telling Kathy that there are fears she cannot understand because she isn't (yet) a donor.

Kathy looks forward to the end of her work as a carer – the unmentioned beginning of donation – and thinks about everything she has lost: Hailsham, Ruth, and now Tommy, who has recently completed. She treasures her memories, though, because no one can take them from her.

# Timeline

The table below sets out an approximation of when the main events occur in the novel. It has to be loose and fluid because Kazuo Ishiguro deliberately keeps the chronology of *Never Let Me Go* free of specific dates.

| Time | What happens |
|---|---|
| Early 1950s | Major medical breakthroughs. Donation programme using clones established. |
| Late 1950s | Miss Emily and Madame establish Hailsham to give 'students' (clones) a relatively normal childhood. |
| Mid to late 1960s | Kathy, Ruth and Tommy born. |
| Late 1960s to early 1980s | Ruth, Kathy and Tommy grow up at Hailsham, from Kathy's first playing a horse game with Ruth, to Ruth's sexual relationship with Tommy. During these years Tommy gradually learns to control his tantrums, Madame collects art, Kathy becomes very attached to a Judy Bridgewater tape, and Miss Lucy spells out the truth about the students' future. **(End of Part One.)** |
| Early 1980s | Kathy, Ruth and Tommy transfer to the Cottages when they're 16. They take a trip to Norfolk with Rodney and Chrissie during their time there. **(End of Part Two.)** |
| Mid-1980s–mid-1990s | Kathy serves 11 years as a carer, during which period both Ruth and Tommy become donors and 'complete'. Between their donations she drives Ruth and Tommy to see a beached boat, and she and Tommy later visit Madame and Miss Emily. |
| Late 1990s | Kathy, now 31, is about to retire as a carer and become a donor. **(End of Part Three.)** |

# Structure of the novel

The novel is presented in 23 chapters and is divided into three parts. It takes the form of the memories and reflections of a single narrator, Kathy. She looks back on her time at Hailsham, from her earliest memories to the time when at 16 she goes to the Cottages, and then on to an 11-year career as a carer, which is soon to end. Part One consists of nine chapters and ends when the students leave Hailsham. Part Two's eight chapters focus on the time at the Cottages and end when Kathy leaves to train as a carer. Part Three has six chapters and takes the narrative though to the present day, when Kathy is about to move on from caring to donation after 11 years as a carer.

That is the framework, but the structure is more complex than that. Ishiguro is aware that human minds wander and digress. Our memories are not organised in tidy packages according to when they happened. In the first chapter, for instance, Kathy begins by describing her present life and work with tantalising mentions in passing of Tommy, Ruth, Hailsham and 'fourth donation', making the reader puzzle over what's going on. Ishiguro's narrative method involves ensuring that nothing is ever spelled out all at once. Information is dropped in gradually as Ishiguro, through his narrator, Kathy, attunes the reader to her situation. She says several times, for example, 'I don't know how it was where you were', as if inviting the reader into the students' world. This opaque form of storytelling compels the reader to read on to make sense of the details as they unfold.

The storytelling is anything but linear. Soon, Ishiguro has Kathy dive back to remember things that happened at Hailsham when she was about twelve. Then in Chapter 2, on page 16, comes mention of being Ruth's carer at Dover only a few years before the present – which triggers memories of Tommy's tantrums, artistic ineptitude, and the ways in which he was bullied at Hailsham. Not until page 45 does the narrator double back in order 'to get down a few things about Ruth, about how we met and became friends, about our early days together.' Her earliest memory of Ruth is of playing with her in the sandpit when they were only five or six years old.

This narrative style sets the pattern for most of the rest of the book, except that there are fewer digressions into the distant past in the latter chapters as she brings her story closer to the present. She unravels her detailed story of their life at Hailsham and what has happened since, moving backwards and forwards in time. The beginning of Chapter 10, for instance, presents Kathy driving between her carer's commitments while reflecting on what they did and didn't do at the Cottages more than eleven years earlier. Even then there are occasional mentions of Hailsham, where – much earlier – she used to play rounders and where she was set an essay to write after leaving.

The novel begins and ends with Kathy aged 31, anticipating her impending retirement as a carer – which is a euphemistic way of acknowledging that her death is approaching. Everything else in the novel sits in the middle, like a huge, apparently untidy, sandwich of random memories. It isn't really untidy or casual, of course. Ishiguro has meticulously arranged every word and every sentence to present to us a frightened woman sharing her past and drip-feeding pieces of terrifying information, rather than organising her thoughts coherently. She has lost everything except her memories, and a terrifying future lies ahead of her. Ishiguro wants us to see that dwelling on her rosy Hailsham memories is part of her way of coping with her lonely situation. The complex storytelling, flashbacks and frequent time shifts give the novel a deceptively disorganised flavour, which is part of the author's characterisation of Kathy as well as a reflection of the nature of memory (see 'Characterisation', p. 33 of this guide).

## GRADE *FOCUS*

### Grade 5

To achieve Grade 5 examiners expect you to show evidence of careful reading and understanding of how Ishiguro structures his story. You will always need to do more than retell the story, but you must show that you know the novel well enough to be able to comment on the author's ideas and views as they are revealed through his methods.

### Grade 8

To achieve this grade you must explore the novel — and the ways in which Ishiguro presents his material — analytically, critically and in detail. Show that you are aware of the many reminiscences and detailed anecdotes that form Kathy's reflections, and the effects that the author creates with them. Don't be afraid to comment on aspects that you find unsuccessful. Choose textual references and quotations carefully and integrate them tightly into your arguments.

## REVIEW YOUR LEARNING

(Answers are given on p. 109.)

1 Why is Kathy allowed to choose some of her donors?

2 Which guardian does Ruth think needs protection?

3 What is the tape that Kathy treasures?

4 What is the name of the community that Ruth, Tommy and Kathy are sent to after Hailsham?

5 Why does Tommy work so hard to produce art after leaving school?

6 Where is the home shared by Miss Emily and Madame?

7 What do you think happened to Kathy's lost tape?

8 What is Chrissie and Rodney's real reason for the Norfolk trip?

9 What is the effect of the Morningdale scandal?

10 Why does Tommy reject Kathy as a carer before his fourth donation?

## Target your thinking

- Who are the key characters in the novel? (**AO1**)
- What techniques does **Kazuo Ishiguro** use to present them? (**AO2**)
- What purposes are served by the characters? (**AO1**, **AO2**, **AO3**)

There are three main characters in *Never Let Me Go*: Kathy, the narrator, and her friends, Ruth and Tommy. All three characters are grappling with suppressed fear of the future but each shows it in a different way.

Beyond them is a handful of people who are also significant, including Miss Emily, Madame, Miss Lucy, Chrissie and Rodney. The other Hailsham students and staff – Laura, Harry and others who are named in passing – are part of the background. Other characters who later feature briefly – such as Mr Keffers who is the link with the outside world for students at the Cottages, and the woman running the Norfolk art gallery – are also part of the background.

## Kathy

Ishiguro opens the novel with Kathy's introduction of herself as Kathy H. This in itself seems a little odd. Why does she not have a surname? This is the first of a series of enigmas that both intrigue and disturb the reader.

As the first person narrator, everything that comes to the reader is filtered through her, except on those occasions when we can see past her – when her tape is stolen and we suspect that Ruth is the culprit, for example, or when we realise that her calm words are her way of controlling her fear of the future and sense of loss.

The writing style is quite informal and chatty, with some use of idiom – for example when she describes another carer as 'a complete waste of space' (p. 3). In this way, Ishiguro begins to create an intimate relationship between narrator and reader, since informal language is a characteristic of speech between friends.

The reader is positioned as someone who is already familiar with the system in which the characters live, as a result of references to 'donors', 'guardians' and 'completing'. It is as if Kathy is addressing the reader as another clone, something that the reader may find disconcerting!

**Key quotation**

*'I don't know how it was where you were, but at Hailsham we had to have some form of medical almost every week...'*
(p. 13)

These matters are spoken about in a very carefully controlled way, allowing little emotion to show. The reader gradually becomes aware of much of what is not being said. For instance, Ishiguro has Kathy state that she is 'looking forward to a bit more companionship come the end of the year when I'm finished with all of this' (p. 232), rather than admitting, even to herself, that she's soon to face the 'ghastly battles' of her own first and subsequent donations.

The reader is told at the outset that Kathy has worked as a carer for 11 years and that this might be seen as an unusually long time. Again, this may seem a little odd. Ishiguro uses a very flat, controlled voice as Kathy tells us that her donors 'have always tended to do better than expected' and that the authorities have been 'pleased with my work, and by and large, I have too' (p. 3). The tone Ishiguro uses here conveys a woman trying to sound very detached, in the style of a medical professional or social worker. It is perhaps a clue to the immense restraint in Kathy's demeanour and the sense of confinement, both physical and psychological, which pervades the novel as a whole.

### Build critical skills

Why might Ishiguro have chosen to have Kathy narrate the story in this way? Are we more likely to trust her attempts at objectivity than we would if the story had been told in a narrative voice full of drama and emotion?

Ishiguro makes it clear that Kathy has watched dozens of people working their way through 'sleepless nights, with the drugs and the pain and exhaustion' (p. 5). Perhaps there is a suggestion that she suffers from 'survivor guilt' – all her friends have gone whereas her competence has extended her own life.

### Build critical skills

'You are a really good carer,' Tommy tells her on page 277. The whole concept of 'caring' in the novel equates to watching others suffering 'ghastly battles' at close quarters, in the certain knowledge that a similar fate awaits the carer. How might we see this as both similar to and different from being an end-of-life carer in our society? What is the effect on the reader?

Now that she is coming to the end of her long stint as a carer, she too will soon become a donor and she knows better than most what that involves. Ishiguro's convoluted storytelling, however, with the flashbacks and digressions that he grants his narrator, makes it clear that all thoughts of that are repressed. Frightened as Ishiguro wants us to realise that she is, he never presents her spelling it out. Instead she talks of looking forward to the rest when she's no longer a carer.

## Build critical skills

How do you react to Kathy's passive acceptance of her fate? What might Ishiguro be suggesting about our own passive acceptance – either of the system in which we live or in our own attitudes to death?

Kathy's mind, as depicted by Ishiguro, is full of her past and what she has lost – perhaps in common with many humans as they approach the end of their lives, and presumably because she is aware that she has no future. She reminisces about the Hailsham years with an awareness that she was privileged to have been there.

Ishiguro presents her in a range of situations, usually positively, although because she is the narrator we only ever see things from Kathy's point of view. For example, he shows us that even as a child she was a good friend, sensitively supporting Ruth when, for example, she lies about her pencil case (p. 56); friendship is clearly valued in this world without parents and families.

She is presented as kind and compassionate, prepared to be different if she thinks it is right, for instance when she reaches out to Tommy when the others are laughing at his tantrum (p. 11). This is the first signal to the reader that Tommy is to be significant in Kathy's life. She is often the peacemaker, trying to calm Tommy (pp. 9–10) and discussing ideas with him, such as those raised by conversations with Miss Lucy about his art.

Ishiguro also suggests she is both perceptive and intelligent. For example, she notices Ruth imitating TV behaviour and rather pitifully copying gestures from the other couples at the Cottages.

Ishiguro makes it clear that his narrator and Tommy have always been drawn to each other, which is why he has Kathy describe her first real encounter with Tommy, during one of his tantrums at Hailsham (p. 11), in such detail. But it is to Ruth that Ishiguro has Tommy eventually turn for a sexual relationship during the final years at Hailsham and when they move to the Cottages. So Kathy becomes an onlooker, sometimes impatient (p. 119), sometimes puzzled (p. 126) and sometimes distressed (p. 164).

Eventually, Ishiguro develops Kathy and Tommy's relationship fully, long after he and Ruth have separated and after Ruth's death. After Tommy's third donation, Kathy becomes his carer and lover, and they allow themselves to hope for a future together. Even when their hopes for a deferral are dashed by Miss Emily (p. 253) Kathy remains, on the surface,

**Key quotation**

*'Maybe come the end of the year when I'm no longer a carer I'll be able to listen to it [her tape] more.'*
(p. 64)

**Key quotation**

*'I lost Ruth, then I lost Tommy, but I won't lose my memories of them. I suppose I lost Hailsham too.'*
(p. 280)

**Key quotation**

*Miss Emily: 'There's no truth in the rumour. I'm sorry. I truly am.'*
(p. 253)

▲ Kathy (right) with Ruth and Tommy in the 2010 film

strangely calm and accepting of the inevitable. Ishiguro clearly contrasts her reaction with that of the more obviously emotional Tommy.

A significant moment is her account of daydreaming while listening to her Judy Bridgewater tape in Chapter 6. Clones like her are physically unable to have children in *Never Let Me Go* but here Kathy, still a child herself, is holding a pillow to her body as if it were a baby. She is fantasising because the words of the song, which she misunderstands due to her lack of experience of the outside world, are 'Baby, baby, never let me go'. She also fails to understand why Madame, who happens to pass the open door, is so moved by what she sees.

Years later, Ishiguro presents Madame explaining what she was really thinking at the time (pp. 266–77). Since Kathy and Madame see this incident from completely different remembered perspectives, Ishiguro seems to be reminding the reader that perception and experience shape memory as much as incidents do.

Ishiguro also hints at Kathy's longing for a sense of her identity in the incident where she searches the pages of a pornographic magazine for her 'possible', and Tommy remarks that she looks 'sad, maybe. And a bit scared.' As she nears the end of her working life we find her clearly wanting to unburden herself of her memories, as Ishiguro guides the reader to contemplate the place of memory in our lives. She thinks that she is reminiscing because of her imminent 'retirement' and credits 'preparing for the change of pace' with her 'urge to order all these old memories' (p. 37).

**Key quotation**

*'…I realise now just how much of what occurred later came out of our time at Hailsham, and that's why I want to go over these earlier memories quite carefully'*
(p. 37)

Her return to Norfolk in the last pages of the novel is extremely moving as she contemplates, within the context of the loss of Tommy, the rubbish and debris caught on the fence.

**Key quotation**

*'I half-closed my eyes and imagined this was the spot where everything I'd lost through my childhood had washed up…'*
(p. 282)

Characteristically, she does not allow herself to lose control, although she tells us that '…the tears rolled down my face', before she resigns herself to her return to wherever she is 'supposed to be' (p. 282).

# Tommy

The first time we meet Tommy in the novel, he is being humiliated by the boys and mocked by Laura in order to entertain the girls (pp. 8–9). Thus Ishiguro presents him as a more vulnerable character and immediately creates sympathy for him in the mind of the reader.

Tommy is presented as a disturbed young boy. He is around twelve at the start of the novel but is given to very dramatic tantrums or 'rages' (p. 10), in which he is seen 'raving, flinging his limbs about at the sky, at the wind, at the nearest fence post.' As such, he reminds us of a much younger child and provides a foil for the more mature and controlled Kathy.

Although these bouts of uncontrollable anger eventually come under control, he regresses towards the end of the novel, by which time he's aged thirty or so. After learning from Miss Emily that there is no hope for the future: '…the second and third screams came … Tommy's figure, raving, shouting, flinging his fists and kicking out … his jumbled swear-words continued uninterrupted' (pp. 268–69). Here again, the reader sympathises with his utter despair. Ishiguro uses Tommy's different way of reacting to adversity as a method of confirming the individuality and therefore the humanity of the students.

Tommy is a hugely important character within the narrative. Ishiguro uses him to highlight the tension that exists at Hailsham between the conflicting veneer of normality in the school and the horrific reality. It is Tommy who has the conversations with Miss Lucy, for example on page 23 wherein she tells him that it doesn't matter if he does not want

**Key quotation**

*"I suppose it is a bit cruel," Ruth said, "the way they always work him up like that."*
(p. 10)

**Key quotation**

*'Then he began to scream and shout, a nonsensical jumble of swear words and insults.'*
(p. 9)

**Build critical skills**

Do you think that there is any significance in Tommy being referred to as Tommy rather than Thomas or Tom? What might Ishiguro have been trying to suggest?

to be creative. This, plus Kathy's incredulous reaction, is an important moment in that it highlights for the reader the sense that Hailsham is a very different school. In later conversation with Miss Lucy, however, she backtracks with little real explanation. Ishiguro further increases the mystique when Tommy tells Kathy what Miss Lucy told him – that there is much about Hailsham and about the wider world that none of them understands.

Again, Tommy is more overt than Kathy and Ruth in trying to work out what the future really holds. He struggles for years, for example, to work out the significance of Madame's Gallery: 'Tommy's big Gallery theory', as Ruth scornfully dismisses it (p. 191).

Ishiguro presents him in a generally positive light. He is clearly sensitive, as even when drawing his tiny animals he worries about how they would protect themselves (p. 185). He is kind and thoughtful towards Kathy, for example in replacing her lost tape in Norfolk (p. 171) and in staying with Kathy when she is upset by Ruth's outburst about the kind of people who would be likely 'possibles'.

Despite his long friendship with Kathy, however, Tommy starts a sexual relationship with Ruth (pp. 92–93). The implication is that Ruth is jealous of Kathy and wants to come between them – and Tommy is weak enough to acquiesce. Although the relationship is far from perfect they drift on as a couple at the Cottages, but the relationship ends when they both move on (p. 213).

Kathy eventually meets up with Tommy again when she and Ruth go to Kingsfield (p. 215), where Tommy is recovering quite well after his third donation. After Ruth's apology and intervention, Tommy and Kathy eventually become a couple. They mistakenly hope that their love might save them, in that they might be allowed to defer.

It is Tommy who raises the spectre of another, more horrific, outcome for clones when he talks about the rumour that after having technically completed, donors remain in some way conscious and that further donations are taken until they are finally switched off.

### Key quotation

*'I'll stay with Kath. If we're splitting, then I'll stay with Kath.'*
(p. 165)

### Key quotation

*'You know why it is Kath, why everyone worries so much about the fourth? It's because they're not sure they'll really complete. If you knew for sure you'd complete, it would be easier. But they never tell us for sure.'*
(p. 273)

Eventually Tommy tells Kathy that he doesn't want her to be his carer during his fourth and final donation. Ultimately he has found the strength to accept his fate and face it alone: 'Kath, I don't want to be that way in front of you' (p. 275).

Their relationship has to end because they now have to accept there is no future (pp. 275–76). Tommy tells her (p. 277) that, 'We've loved each other all our lives. But in the end, we can't stay together forever.' This is one of the most poignant and perceptive sentences in the novel because it's a universal truth. We are all – eventually – separated by death from those we love.

## Key quotation

*'I keep thinking about this river somewhere, with the water moving really fast. And these two people in the water, trying to hold onto each other, holding on as hard as they can, but in the end it's just too much. The current's too strong. They've got to let go, drift apart. That's how it is with us.'*
(p. 277)

# Ruth

Our first impression of Ruth is somewhat negative as she is seen laughing at the unsuspecting Tommy, without any sign of disapproval of what the boys were about to do to him. Ishiguro contrasts her reaction with that of Kathy, who does at least feel 'a stab of pain' and who later goes to his aid.

Ruth becomes a close friend of Kathy's when they are both very young at Hailsham. Kathy has a memory of playing with her once in the sandpit but not of playing with her again properly until Ruth allows her to play an imaginary horse game (pp. 46–47): 'You can ride Bramble ... But you're not to use your crop on him. And you've got to come *now*' (p. 46).

We immediately see Ruth being bossy and manipulative here, allowing Kathy to play only on Ruth's terms. This foreshadows her later domination and manipulation of others, particularly Tommy. Her overbearing manner is, perhaps, her way of covering unspoken inner fears and anxieties about the future.

Ishiguro also shows us here that Ruth has the imagination of any ordinary child at play – an important point in a novel that asks what it is that makes us fully human. We see the same thing a few pages later when Ruth imagines that one of the Hailsham guardians, Miss Geraldine, is in some sort of danger and so takes control, mustering a group of children to be her secret guard.

She is in many ways a complex character. This is articulated by Kathy, who refers to Ruth as having two sides to her personality. 'One Ruth ... always trying to impress veterans ... putting on airs and pretending' and 'Ruth from Hailsham ... who sat beside me in my little attic room at the day's close' (p. 127).

## Key quotation

*'And Ruth had been at her best: encouraging, funny, tactful, wise.'*
(p. 126)

At times, Ishiguro shows us a damaged and emotionally deprived child with human needs, suggesting that she is desperately in need of love and attention, for example when she pretends that her pencil case is a gift from Miss Geraldine (p. 56). He also reveals her vulnerability through her distress when she realises that Kathy knows the truth about the pencil case (pp. 59–60).

▲ What use does Ruth make of her pencil case?

We may also feel some sympathy towards her as she is clearly lacking in confidence. She pretends she can play chess (p. 52); a more self-assured, less needy child would admit that she couldn't. Later, in Chapter 11, she pretends to have read certain books for the same reason.

Sometimes she appears capable of being a good friend and we empathise with her longing to find her 'possible' during the trip to Norfolk.

Ishiguro, however, also depicts a darker side to Ruth. She is filled with self-loathing as she believes that all clones are products of rejected members of society. This awareness brings her close to angry despair as Ishiguro reveals her true feelings, to the discomfort of those around her. 'We're modelled from *trash*. Junkies, prostitutes, winos, tramps. Convicts maybe, just as long as they aren't psychos' (p. 164).

Perhaps it is this belief that feeds her cruel and destructive tendencies. These are often shown through her treatment of the gentle Tommy or through some of her vicious remarks to Kathy, such as when she betrays her confidence and throws her sex life back at her.

Her sexual relationship with Tommy is embarked upon mainly to keep him and Kathy apart (pp. 92–93), despite her awareness that, from childhood, there has been a bond between Tommy and Kathy. Later, at the Cottages, Ishiguro highlights her continuing instability as she sometimes makes efforts to draw Kathy in (in the car on the way back from Norfolk in Chapter 15, for example), while at other times being brittle and dismissive. 'So that's it, that's what's upsetting poor little Kathy. Ruth isn't paying enough attention to her' (p. 122). For most of the novel, the reader may feel that it is very difficult to like her.

## Key quotation

*'So that's it, that's what's upsetting poor little Kathy. Ruth isn't paying enough attention to her. Ruth's got big new friends and baby sister isn't getting played with so often...'*
(p. 122)

After she leaves the Cottages Kathy loses contact with Ruth for several years, until she hears that Ruth has had a 'bad first donation' and is in a recovery centre in Dover. She volunteers to be Ruth's carer, a somewhat unsatisfactory and awkward experience for both until they meet up with Tommy again in order to go and see a boat. During this expedition, Ishiguro highlights Ruth's frailty as well as her genuine desire for forgiveness and redemption.

## Key quotation

*'And almost as an instinct, we both went to her. I took an arm, Tommy supported her elbow on the other side, and we began gently guiding her towards the fence.'*
(p. 218)

Here Ishiguro creates some sympathy for Ruth, who has thought long, hard and regretfully over the past and now wants Kathy and Tommy to get together and seek a deferral. She has even gone to the trouble of obtaining Madame's address for them (p. 229). Shortly afterwards, Ruth undergoes her second donation (p. 231), and the reader cannot help feeling pity as Kathy observes her struggling to 'patrol and marshal all the better the separate areas of pain in her body' as she lies dying (p. 231).

### GRADE BOOSTER

```
Always remember that the characters in the novel have
been created by a writer and that your focus needs to
be on the ways that the writer has made the characters
come alive for the reader. Don't write about the
characters as if they were real people. If the words
'Ishiguro' or 'the writer' don't appear several times
in your answer you are probably not answering the
question and you are unlikely to achieve high marks.
```

# Miss Emily

Miss Emily is the Head Guardian at Hailsham and as such she disappears from the novel at the end of Chapter 9, when Kathy, Ruth and Tommy leave. She reappears at the end in Chapters 21 and 22 when Kathy and Ruth find her, now disabled, living with Madame in Littlehampton.

In the early stages, Ishiguro presents Miss Emily primarily as quite a strict figure who instils fear in the students. It is made clear, however, that the students see Miss Emily as 'fair', as revealed by her even-handed approach to the 'tokens question' (p. 39), and Kathy says that they 'respected her decisions' (p. 39).

▲ Charlotte Rampling as Miss Emily in the 2010 film

Miss Emily does much of the teaching at Hailsham herself and is completely unfazed by the details of sex education in the classroom (p. 82). She uses a skeleton to demonstrate the 'nuts and bolts of how you did it' (p. 82), but Ishiguro reveals a different side to her nature when she warns the students of the emotional dangers of promiscuity.

Ishiguro gives the reader a number of hints that Miss Emily is more than simply an authority figure, such as the descriptions of her 'wandering round Hailsham in a dream, talking to herself' (p. 43) and her unusual behaviour in some assemblies (p. 43).

**Build critical skills**

Look carefully at the description of Miss Emily's hairstyle on page 39. What might Ishiguro be suggesting about her character through this description?

**GRADE** *BOOSTER*

Don't forget the importance of 'reading between the lines'. Look out for examples of Kathy failing to see the 'bigger picture' in her references to Miss Emily. Don't fall into the same trap!

It is only in Chapter 22 that a fuller picture of Miss Emily emerges for both Kathy and the reader. It transpires that she was part of an experiment in providing cloned children with high quality education and giving them a protected and happy childhood before they have to become donors: the aim was to provide 'an example of how we might move to a more humane and better way of doing things' (p. 253).

By this stage of the novel Hailsham and the small number of other similar schools have closed and been replaced by 'vast, government "homes"' (p. 260), which Miss Emily clearly disapproves of. She and Marie-Claude are deeply in debt as a result of the loss of the money they sank into Hailsham.

Ishiguro presents Miss Emily as a woman with altruistic motives, who perhaps represents those who believe young people should be sheltered from the harsh truths of life. She addresses Tommy and Kathy quite gently as 'my dears' (p. 252) and tells them that, at Hailsham, they were 'kept away from the worst of those horrors' (p. 256) and that they have had the privilege of growing up with education and culture.

## Key quotation

*'I did all the worrying and questioning for the lot of you. And as long as I was steadfast, then no doubts ever crossed your mind.'*
(p. 255)

# Madame (Marie-Claude)

Although the children do not realise it while they're at the school, because they see Madame only on her occasional visits, she and Miss Emily had founded Hailsham and run it jointly. Ishiguro presents both as characters who believe that young clones should be treated much better than they usually are within the wider world of *Never Let Me Go*, and they use the students' art to try to prove that the clones have 'souls'.

## Key quotation

*'We took away your art because we thought it would reveal your souls. Or to put it more finely, we did it to prove you had souls at all.'*
(p. 255)

Madame collects the best of the children's art and takes it away to a place the Hailsham students among themselves call her 'Gallery', although they rarely discuss it with adults. The children believe that Madame is afraid of them and Ishiguro clearly portrays her revulsion when she 'froze' in their presence.

## Key quotation

*'...she was afraid of us in the way someone might be afraid of spiders.'*
(p. 263)

Ishiguro also allows the reader a glimpse into a more sympathetic side of Madame when she witnesses Kathy dancing with her pillow and singing 'Never let me go'. Madame is clearly moved by what she sees and the reader is shown that she does have some compassion for the clones.

Later in the novel, Kathy and Tommy find Madame and Miss Emily sharing a home, apparently as partners. Miss Emily addresses Madame, whom she calls Marie-Claude, as 'darling'. The remnants of Madame's Gallery are now in the Littlehampton house. Madame is shown now to be Miss Emily's carer and Ishiguro presents her as appearing bitter towards the clones, perhaps in some way blaming them for the situation she now finds herself in.

Although Madame says very little in this section she does explain to Kathy why she was moved by her dancing to her tape all those years previously: 'I saw a little girl, her eyes tightly closed, holding to her breast the kind old world, one that she knew in her heart could not remain, and she was holding it and pleading, never to let her go' (p. 267).

Through Kathy's eyes Madame often appears unfeeling, but Ishiguro presents her in a more complex way. Her final words, 'Poor creatures', suggest both sympathy and also a failure to see the clones as human. Miss Emily, however, has no doubt as to Madame's true nature.

**Key quotation**

*'she just went on standing out there, sobbing and sobbing…'*
(p. 71)

**Key quotation**

*'…she remained standing behind the wheelchair, her eyes blazing towards us.'*
(p. 250)

**Key quotation**

*'Poor creatures. I wish I could help you. But now you're by yourselves.'*
(p. 267)

**Key quotation**

*'Marie-Claude has given everything for you. She has worked and worked and worked. Make no mistake about it. Marie-Claude is on your side and will always be on your side.'*
(pp. 263–64)

# Miss Lucy

Miss Lucy is a young Hailsham guardian who comes to believe that it is wrong for the students to be raised in ignorance of their fate. 'You've been told and not told' (p. 79) she declares, with some justification, because the children have a lot of sketchy knowledge of things that have been mentioned in passing but not made clear. In this way, Ishiguro uses her as a contrast to Miss Emily, who prefers to shelter the students from the unpleasant realities of their future.

**Key quotation**

*'You've been told and not told…'*
(p. 79)

**Key quotation**

*Miss Emily on Miss Lucy: 'She thought you students had to be made more aware. More aware of what lay ahead of you, who you were, what you were for.'*
(p. 262)

Kathy sees her in her study, clearly angry about something, and both Kathy and the reader gradually become aware that she is beset by 'worries and frustrations'. For example, she tells Tommy that art does not matter, and then years later tells him to forget what she said and that art *is* important because it is 'evidence'. Although this confuses Tommy and Kathy, it prepares the reader for the truth when it is revealed to them at the end of the novel by Madame.

Eventually Miss Lucy tells them the truth quite plainly. Soon after that she is dismissed from the school. 'Lucy Wainwright was idealistic. Nothing wrong with that…' explains Miss Emily, years later (p. 262). 'Lucy was well-meaning enough. But if she'd had her way your happiness at Hailsham would have been shattered. … So she had to go' (p. 263).

Miss Lucy is a significant character in Ishiguro's creation because her feelings and desire for honesty seem, on the surface, much more acceptable and 'normal' to the reader. She is presented by Ishiguro in direct contrast to the other guardians, who do not challenge the ways of Hailsham, and so Lucy might be seen as an attractive, rebellious character. The reader, however, is perhaps also being asked to judge whether honesty is always the best policy.

Within the narrative Miss Lucy also provides clues as to what is really going on and therefore her presence contributes to the reader's sense of creeping unease.

## Miss Geraldine

Miss Geraldine is described by Kathy as 'everyone's favourite guardian' (p. 19) and she is presented by Ishiguro as the most maternal of the guardians, offering comfort and support to the children. Geraldine becomes the focus of the girls' attention as shown by Ruth's 'secret guard', which she forms to protect her.

### Build critical skills

The guardians Emily, Lucy and Geraldine are presented in very different ways. What purpose do you think each one serves within the novel? Do you think Ishiguro wants the reader to sympathise with any one of them in particular?

Interestingly, Ishiguro suggests that Geraldine's kindly approach might not always be successful, as the resentment towards Tommy is linked with her 'praise' of his immature artwork (p. 20).

### Key quotation

*Tommy to Kathy: 'I think Miss Lucy was right. Not Miss Emily.'* (p. 168)

### GRADE BOOSTER

Ishiguro's characters do not fit into simple categories. Offering alternative interpretations will lead to higher grades!

# Chrissie and Rodney

Chrissie and Rodney are an established couple at the Cottages. They are a little older than Kathy, Ruth and Tommy and are part of a group known as 'the veterans'. Ishiguro raises our suspicions about them because of Kathy's comment only a few weeks after meeting Chrissie that she felt she was 'up to something' (p. 139).

As they function mainly as a device, their characters are sketchily drawn – just a couple in their late teens or early twenties, who are in love but will be unable to fulfil a married life together. One of the ways that Ishiguro foregrounds the idea of Chrissie's duplicity is through Kathy's comment that although Chrissie was quite beautiful, she tried to minimise her height by crouching down, making her look 'more like the Wicked Witch than a movie star' (p. 139). Kathy sees Rodney as 'pretty much under Chrissie's influence' (p. 139).

Key quotation

*'You'd hardly ever see Chrissie without her boyfriend Rodney.'*
(p. 139)

They are used to highlight Ruth's lack of confidence as she clearly admires them, even imitating some of their mannerisms and gestures. They take advantage of her naivety and her dreams, however, by encouraging her to accompany them to Cromer, on the pretext of seeing her 'possible'.

More importantly, however, they are used to introduce the idea of deferrals, an idea that will become important later in the novel. Clinging desperately to the slim hope of a slightly extended future together, they have heard rumours that it is possible for Hailsham students, if they can prove they are in love, to have their donations put back by a few years. The trip to Norfolk is an opportunity to quiz Ruth about this rumour (p. 150), but Ishiguro also uses it to highlight the tragic situation of all the clones. The fact that Ruth is not honest with them does not impress Kathy – or indeed the reader.

Key quotation

*'...the people who run Hailsham, they sorted it out for you. They sorted it out so you could have a few years together before you began your donations.'*
(p. 151)

We later hear that Chrissie 'completes' during her second donation (p. 221) while Rodney is in a centre in North Wales, where Kathy happens to meet him, having not seen Chrissie for 'a couple of years' (p. 222).

# Other characters

## Keffers

At the Cottages, Keffers is the taciturn 'grumpy old guy' (p. 114) who comes two or three times each week to inspect the place and bring supplies. He is really their only regular link with the outside world and is therefore used by Ishiguro to indicate negative attitudes towards clones. It is he who processes the paperwork when Kathy decides to begin her carer training (p. 199).

## Laura

Kathy meets a Hailsham/Cottages friend, Laura, later when Laura is finding her work as a carer very stressful (pp. 205–07). She is used by Ishiguro to provide another dimension to the role that Kathy generally makes light of. It is Laura who reports to Kathy that Ruth has suffered a bad first donation.

## Harry C.

Harry C. is a Hailsham boy whom Kathy plans to have sex with (p. 96), although this never actually happens. He is useful to confirm the very matter-of-fact attitude to sex that Kathy shares with the other students – and perhaps the complete lack of a sense of the sacred nature of one's body. Years later she meets Harry, by then quite ill, in a recovery centre in Wiltshire (p. 99) and doesn't think he recognises her. For the reader, he acts as another reminder of the fate that awaits Kathy, Tommy and Ruth.

## GRADE *FOCUS*

### Grade 5

To achieve Grade 5 you will need to show a clear understanding of how Ishiguro presents characters using language, form and structure. You'll need to consider what ideas Ishiguro might be suggesting about a character and to use textual references to support a range of points.

### Grade 8

To achieve this grade you will examine and evaluate the ways that Ishiguro presents characters through language, form and structure. You will explore both implicit and explicit ideas about characters and will recognise that more than one interpretation is possible. Supporting textual references will be precise, apt and well integrated into the response.

## REVIEW YOUR LEARNING

(Answers are given on p. 110.)

**1** How does Ishiguro suggest that Kathy's life might be a little strange in the first sentence of the novel?

**2** What incident at the start of the novel does Ishiguro use to suggest that Tommy is vulnerable?

**3** What aspect of Ruth's character is revealed during the incident when the children are playing at riding a horse?

**4** How does Ishiguro create sympathy for Ruth at the end of her life?

**5** What is the main function of Rodney and Chrissie in the novel?

**6** How does Miss Geraldine's popularity reveal itself?

**7** Which guardian believes the students should be told the whole truth about their futures, and why?

**8** What is the significance of Ruth's lies about her pencil case?

**9** What is the reason for Tommy's rage after the visit to Miss Emily?

**10** At the very end of the novel, why might Kathy's return to whatever it was she was 'supposed to be doing' seem rather bleak?

# Target your thinking

- What are the novel's main themes? (**AO1**)
- What do they add to the novel? (**AO1**, **AO2**, **AO3**)
- How do themes work? (**AO2**)

A theme is an idea, or a set of ideas, threaded through a piece of writing. Think of *Never Let Me Go* as a piece of multi-coloured fabric. A theme is a single-coloured thread – red, blue, yellow and so on. Each thread is woven into the whole as part of the pattern. It mixes with the other colours that it crosses to make shapes or new colours. All the threads overlap. In the same way, Kazuo Ishiguro weaves together his ideas about respect for humanity, growing up, relationships, death and more into the story that he is telling.

When we discuss a theme, it is as if we are pulling out a single thread from the novel's overall pattern. We can look at it on its own and then weave it back into the whole.

The themes in *Never Let Me Go* that we will consider here are:

- humanity
- death
- fear
- education
- friendship
- love
- loss.

Remember the following three points as you think about the themes in this novel:

1  No theme in a novel is completely separate from any other. They all overlap to create a whole. That is what makes a text such as *Never Let Me Go* feel complete.

2  In examination questions, similar themes are often referred to using different names. For example friendship is close to attachment, comradeship or close relationships. Learning is close to education and, in the world of *Never Let Me Go*, to art or artistic development. Do not get too carried away with compiling long, repetitive lists of themes.

**3** Some themes feature more regularly than others in the pattern of the novel.

# Humanity

Can you be a fully developed human being if you are an artificially created, parentless clone whose sole function is to provide organs for 'real' people with diseases? Ishiguro presents his children playing normally, needing praise and encouragement, and yearning for individual adult love (that's why Ruth wants the others to think she's Miss Geraldine's favourite, pp. 56–57). They engage in the usual petty jealousies and each child is different – as they would be in a traditional orphanage where children live together in a parentless world. Ruth, Tommy and Kathy seem like any other children.

## Key quotation

*Miss Emily: 'Here was the world, requiring students to donate. While that remained the case, there would always be a barrier against the world seeing you as properly human.'*
(p. 258)

Later they are informed about sex (pp. 81–82) and encouraged to have sex when they feel like it (pp. 94–97). Some of them (Chrissie and Rodney, p. 151, and eventually Kathy and Tommy, p. 247) discover that complicated feelings of attachment and love come with that. They may be unable to have children but they can fall in love just like anyone else. Ishiguro is suggesting that these experiences are characteristics of all human beings. His clones may be a sort of sub-class in the world he has created, but emotionally and spiritually they equal anyone else.

The unseen authorities in *Never Let Me Go* seem happy enough for the clones to live their lives more or less as they wish – at the Cottages for instance – including having the freedom to explore the 'outside' if they want to, until the time comes first to work as a carer and then for donation. At that point, relationships and needs are cruelly disregarded. We hear, for example, that the donation programme has separated Chrissie and Rodney and sent them to different centres (pp. 221–22).

Meanwhile, Miss Emily and Madame have worked hard to give their Hailsham students a humane childhood. But it was an experiment, in which Miss Emily tells Kathy and Tommy they were 'lucky pawns' (p. 261). 'We've given you better lives than you would have had otherwise', she observes as she tells Kathy and Tommy about students being raised in 'deplorable conditions' now that Hailsham and the handful of comparable schools have been closed.

Even Miss Emily, however, is presented as finding her cloned charges repulsive – presumably because she regards them as unnatural and subhuman. 'We're *all* afraid of you. I myself had to fight back my dread of you almost every day I was at Hailsham. There were times when I'd look down at you all from my study window and feel such revulsion...' (p. 264).

In the past people used slaves, unseen by most Europeans, to produce sugar, which was as economically important in the eighteenth century as oil is today. In the twenty-first century millions work for very low wages in 'sweatshops' in, for example, India, largely ignored by most people in the developed world who wear the clothes they produce. 'The world didn't want to be reminded how the donation programme really worked', Miss Emily tells Tommy and Kathy (p. 259).

## Build critical skills

The clones are deprived of human rights because their lives are seen as being of less value. How might Ishiguro be exploring ideas about how people who are perceived as being different are treated? Can you think of groups of people, either historically or in the present, who have been treated as less than human?

# Death

The students in *Never Let Me Go* are destined to die while still in their twenties and thirties. There are no deferrals and no room for negotiation. 'Your life must now run the course which has been set out for it', as Miss Emily tells Ruth and Tommy (p. 261).

## Key quotation

*Miss Lucy to the children: 'Your lives are set out for you. You'll become adults, then before you're old, before you're even middle-aged, you'll start to donate your vital organs. That's what each of you was created to do.'*
(p. 80)

In a sense then, impending death hangs over every student, although they live in denial of it most of the time. They talk of recovery centres and people being well – as if there were a future. Tommy, for example, mentions a donor he knows, saying, 'But it all turned out fine. He's just come through his third now and he's completely all right' (p. 223). Clearly the reader is meant to notice this and recognise that, behind Tommy's bravado, he is talking of a person who has just donated vital organs for the third time and whose next trip to the operating theatre will end in certain death, so he can't possibly be 'completely all right'.

> **Key quotation**
>
> *Tommy: 'You and me, right from the start, even when we were little, we were always trying to find things out. Remember, Kath, all those secret talks we used to have? But Ruth wasn't like that. She always wanted to believe in things.'*
> (p. 278)

The language given to the donors to discuss all this supports this avoidance of the blunt truth. Rather than dying, characters 'complete' (their lives). Only once in the whole novel does Ishiguro allow a character to mention the stark reality. On page 254, when Kathy is very distressed as she realises that there really is no hope of an alternative future, she blurts out: 'If we're just going to give donations anyway, then die, why all those lessons?'

### Build critical skills

*Never Let Me Go* uses 'completion' as a euphemism for death. Jot down a quick list of five real-life euphemisms for death, such as 'passing away' or 'pushing up the daisies'. Why do human beings hide behind this sort of language? What is Ishiguro suggesting about those who control the main characters by encouraging them to avoid frank terms to describe their future?

## A parable about mortality?

Some critics have suggested that *Never Let Me Go* is not really about clones and organ donation at all. Ishiguro has simply, they argue, used a loosely contrived science fiction setting to examine human attitudes to death. If so, this would help to explain why the details are not realistic; the novel isn't intended to be realistic because it's a parable about mortality.

A parable is a story that explains or teaches a point, such as the parable of the prodigal son in the Bible (Luke 15: 11–32), the details of which are not realistic either. Aesop's fables, for example about the boy who cried wolf, are other examples.

Death awaits all human beings and there is little we can do to control how and when it happens. In the novel, however, it awaits the clones in a specific and calculated way.

The children growing up at Hailsham are protected from too much knowledge about death – just as most people in real life would discuss it with children in general terms without, probably, dwelling too much on the details. Thus, like the Hailsham students, many real children are 'told but not told', as Miss Lucy puts it (p. 81) in *Never Let Me Go*. If children – in the novel or in life – were relentlessly taught that they were simply growing up in order to die, then – as Miss Emily observes (pp. 254–55) – they would, quite reasonably, question the point of being educated or trying to live well.

All religions offer some sort of positive explanation of death in order to enable their believers to hope and to face the future without fear or despair. People who don't have these beliefs somehow have to face the future knowing that their life will end completely, possibly after being 'all hooked up' (p. 5) and with plenty of 'drugs, and the pain and the exhaustion' (p. 5). The rumours and stories that spread among the students – especially of possible deferral – could, if we accept the mortality parable analysis, represent a religion of hope in *Never Let Me Go*. In the end, what ultimately makes this such a dark novel is that Tommy and Kathy are denied all such hope when Miss Emily tells them the blunt truth, that 'your life must now run the course which has been set for it' (p. 261).

By having Tommy send Kathy away when he finally accepts that he will soon die and there is no alternative future (p. 275), Ishiguro is representing Tommy's recognition that he will need to face death alone. In real life, relationships change and sometimes become more distant as one person is gradually swallowed up by illness and death while the other goes on living. Like Kathy, many people approach death with a frightened acceptance of the inevitable that is best not thought about too deeply – however much dying they have witnessed. She is, perhaps, similar to a very elderly person who has lived long but has gradually over the years lost many loved ones.

One view might be that Ishiguro's searingly bleak novel actually invites the reader to develop a healthier and more open attitude to death, or at least to reflect on different attitudes to it.

## Fear

All the students presented by Ishiguro in *Never Let Me Go* face a terrifying future. Miss Emily and her staff shelter them from having to think about it too truthfully while they are at Hailsham, but they are fairly aware of what lies ahead once they reach the Cottages. The novel is, in part, an exploration of acceptance and/or denial of that which faces every human being.

### Key quotation

*'Because it doesn't really matter how well your guardians prepare you: all the talks, videos, discussions, warnings, none of that can really bring it home.'* (p. 36)

This fear, we are meant to infer, comes out in different ways in different characters in the novel, as it does in real life. It makes Tommy prone to uncontrollable rages. It causes Ruth to do a lot of pretending and posturing – e.g. that she can play chess (pp. 52–53) or that as a Hailsham student she has privileged knowledge that Chrissie doesn't (p. 152) – as well as to be overbearing to other people. It makes Kathy strive so hard to suppress what she's really feeling that she communicates in an unnaturally careful flat voice: 'I should explain why I got so bothered by Ruth saying what she did' (p. 124) and that repeated, cautious, 'I don't know how it was where you were, but...' (p. 13 and elsewhere). The effect of this is to make the reader consider how all human beings manage their fear.

## Key quotation

*'Maybe all of us at Hailsham had little secrets like that – little private nooks created out of thin air where we could go off alone with our fears and longings.'*
(p. 73)

## Key quotation

*'I get to see a lot as a carer. An awful lot.'*
(p. 222)

Kathy has worked for 11 years as a carer and has seen many donors reach 'completion', a chilling euphemism for death. Every donor has worked as a carer before becoming a donor, but Kathy's stint has been longer than most, as she explains at the opening of the novel. This means that all donors know precisely what faces them at the point when they embark on first donation.

Kathy has seen a great deal of sickness, suffering and death and knows that an identical fate awaits her at the end of the year. Ishiguro doesn't need to have her tell us how frightened she is.

Chrissie and Rodney are terrified of their future too, although it is presented slightly more distantly as they are outside the central three characters. The reader notices how Chrissie's voice is 'wobbling slightly' (p. 152) when she first finds the courage to ask Ruth, Tommy and Kathy if they know anything from Hailsham that could help them. They are, Kathy realises, troubled by a 'notion which fascinated, and nagged and scared them' (p. 163).

At the end of the novel Ishiguro moves the reader deeply by making it clear that it's partly Tommy's fear – his fourth donation papers have arrived – which allows him to find the dignity to send away the devastated Kathy. He is frightened, we infer, of the effect that sharing 'this last bit' will have on the love they feel for each other. They talk a lot during the weeks before the final goodbye (p. 278), like any other couple openly facing separation and death.

Ishiguro shows us Kathy controlling most of her feelings tightly to the last: 'I wasn't sobbing or out of control' (p. 282). She convinces herself that she is looking forward to stopping her work as a carer, as if it were going to be a happy, peaceful retirement. In fact, she will soon go into first donation – alone and fearful apart from an assigned professional carer. Because she has been reprieved for so long, most of her friends have long since completed. She allows herself a little fantasy and a few tears on page 282, and then turns to face her bleak and frightening future. It is a chilly end to the novel, as Ishiguro intends it to be.

## Key quotation

'... *and although the tears rolled down my face, I wasn't sobbing or out of control. I just waited a bit, then turned back to the car to drive off to wherever it was I was supposed to be.*'
(p. 282)

# Education

Ishiguro's Hailsham students are nurtured, educated and given a fairly normal, if institutionalised, childhood. They read books, create art and enjoy music. We infer that this is probably not the norm even within the compass of *Never Let Me Go*. Life at Hailsham is very different from that at 'other vast government "homes"'; Miss Emily tells Kathy and Tommy (p. 260) that it would stop them sleeping for days if they saw what went on in some of those places. 'At this very moment there are students being reared in deplorable conditions you Hailsham students could hardly imagine. And now we're no more, things will only get worse' (p. 255). On page 5 Kathy mentions a donor she cared for who'd been at 'some place in Dorset' of which he desperately 'didn't want to be reminded'. Equally, Ishiguro may intend the reader to reflect on education in real life and to consider the importance of the arts in education and in the development of rounded human beings – quite a topical worry in the twenty-first century amid funding cuts. Similarly, Hailsham students are, in a sense, like imprisoned animals, never allowed to go beyond the grounds. It means they are very restricted in their outlook and experience. This too could be a comment on the limited nature of education in the real world today.

Miss Emily, Madame and their colleagues (apart from Miss Lucy) believe that education, art and culture will enrich the lives of the students and make them better people, irrespective of their future early death. This is, effectively, an argument in favour of education for its own sake rather than as preparation for, for example, a career. Miss Lucy tells them bluntly on page 80 that none of them will have a career. Nonetheless, the Hailsham view is that however short your life, you will live it better if you are well educated. 'Why all those books and discussions?' asks Kathy (p. 254) when she's trying to make sense of the Hailsham ethos now that she knows there is no hope of a deferral. Miss Emily explains (p. 263) that she and the other guardians deliberately sheltered students from the dreadful truth in order to allow them to have childhoods.

**Build critical skills**

'You've had good lives, you're educated and cultured' (Miss Emily, p. 256). What value does education have beyond school itself? To what extent is this devalued by the characters' limited lifespans?

The counter-argument that Ishiguro invites us to consider is that by keeping people in ignorance through not educating them, they will not have many expectations or want to ask questions. When Kathy and Tommy decide to approach Madame for help with a deferral at the end of the novel they are using the power of reasoning, which their good education has bred in them. It is easier for the authorities if people don't ask questions. Hailsham, which taught its students to think, has long since closed. Ishiguro shows that options for free thinking are disappearing as attitudes change and time passes – in real life as in the novel.

At Hailsham the educational emphasis seems to be on art ('We took your art away because we thought it would reveal your souls', p. 255), writing, music and the humanities, such as geography (pp. 64–65) and history (p. 77). There is also plenty of sport and a certain amount of preparation for life, including graphic sex education (p. 82). It's a very protective, selective form of education, bearing in mind that in the real world education is a preparation for life. Yes, Hailsham teaches its students the things they will need to know when they are able to visit the 'outside', but carefully avoids telling them most of what will happen to them.

**Key** quotation

*"There, look!" we could say. "Look at this art! How dare you claim these children are anything less than fully human?"'*
(p. 256)

▲ Art is treated as important at Hailsham

# Friendship

Kathy and Ruth become friends. Tommy and Kathy are close friends too. In both cases the friendship starts in infancy and lasts until death, with a ten-year gap in the middle. These friendships are very intense and often troubled, partly because the children have no families, and there is a generally friendly bonding between Kathy and the other Hailsham students. Note, for example, her relationship with the distressed Laura when they're both working as carers years later (pp. 204–08).

## Ruth

Kathy's friendship with Ruth is presented as close but often awkward. Kathy really cares about how Ruth feels. She is deeply sorry, for instance, when she realises how much she has upset Ruth by showing her up over the provenance of the special pencil case (pp. 59–60), and she treasures a tape that Ruth gave her as 'one of my most precious possessions' (p. 75). On the other hand, Ruth is temperamentally quite a difficult person, who sneers often at Kathy: 'Oh look who's upset now. Poor Kathy. She never likes straight talking' (p. 165).

Ruth is clearly jealous of Kathy's friendship with Tommy, although pretty cruel and matter-of-fact about his outbursts. 'It's his own fault. If he learned to keep his cool, they'd leave him alone' (p. 10). Towards the end of her life she admits some of this and asks for Kathy's forgiveness. 'I kept you and Tommy apart ... that was the worst thing I did ... I'm not pretending I didn't always see that ... of course I did' (p. 228). We may be meant, as readers, to suspect that Ruth, perhaps because of her parent-free upbringing, is not capable of unconditional love or friendship.

## Tommy

At Hailsham Kathy is the only child who tries to help and support Tommy when he is having a tantrum or being quite nastily bullied by others. This leads to trust developing between them and to conversations in which they confide in each other – on page 23, for example, and later on page 134 when he finds her leafing through pornographic magazines at the Cottages, or during the trip to Norfolk in Chapter 15. Ishiguro presents the Kathy/Tommy friendship as one that matures into adult life until, much later, after Tommy's third donation, it becomes a sexual relationship (p. 234).

Ishiguro wants the reader to understand that friendship can take different forms and, perhaps, to notice that three-way friendships are liable to be difficult under any circumstances.

**Key quotation**

*Cynthia E. to Kathy: 'And Tommy. I knew it wouldn't last with Ruth. Well, I suppose you're the natural successor.'* (p. 98)

**Build critical skills**

How well do you think the title of the novel suits the subject matter?

## Miss Emily and Madame

Notice the other main friendship in the novel too. Miss Emily and Madame have been drawn together by a common purpose and shared views. At the end of the novel they are sharing a home, perhaps as a couple, and Madame is supporting her disabled friend/partner by, for example, dealing with the man from the decorating company (p. 253) and supervising the men who come to take the bedside cabinet (p. 263).

# Love

Ishiguro presents love in several forms in *Never Let Me Go*, although it is rarely mentioned by name. Note that in real life love is usually first experienced at home between parents and children. None of Ishiguro's clones has this as a starting point. They can't be expected to understand any form of love properly if they have never been given any.

## Fraternal love

'We have loved each other all our lives', Ishiguro has Tommy tell Kathy on page 277. The way in which they are drawn together and trust each other as children suggests the sort of protective fraternal love you find between brother and sister. And it's something neither of them ever quite achieves with touchy, volatile Ruth with her quick and unpredictable recourse to sneering put-downs – not as a child, a young adult or even when she's quite ill (p. 222, for example). Under her brittle manner, Ruth probably does feel real sisterly love for Kathy. Why else does she want Kathy's forgiveness and a means to right the wrong she now admits (p. 228) she's done the other two?

**Key quotation**

*'All the guardedness, all the suspicions between me and Ruth evaporated, and we seemed to remember everything we'd once meant to each other.'*
(p. 230)

## Sexual love

Sex and love are not the same thing in *Never Let Me Go*. Sex cannot, as it sometimes does in real life, lead to the birth of children. Ishiguro is, perhaps, inviting the reader to reflect on the relationship between sex and procreation, as real life medical science continuously finds ways of separating them.

Ruth and Tommy have sex and become a couple; it seems to be a relationship of convenience and neither of them ever claims to love the other. They are quite different from Chrissie and Rodney, a straightforward conventional couple who seem to be deeply in love. Chrissie struggles to articulate this on page 151: 'if you were a boy and a girl, and you were in love with each other, really, properly in love, and if you could show it…'. Kathy, Ruth and Tommy speculate (p. 221) about what it would have been like for distressed Rodney after Chrissie's premature completion in a clinic miles away from his own recovery centre. Chrissie and Rodney's relationship provides a comparison and contrast with that of Ruth and Tommy.

Kathy, meanwhile, decides that it's time she started to have sex (p. 96) and thinks about suggesting this to Harry C. (p. 97). She is frightened of her own sexuality and urges, and fears that she may have acquired them by being modelled from a pornographic model, for example (p. 179). Later at the Cottages she has a few 'one-nighters'. These are casual and functional, partly born of curiosity, and have nothing to do with love or affection. It isn't until her relationship with Tommy changes (p. 234) that her emotions become involved. Even then she describes what happens very mechanically, without mentioning love. She pretends to herself that she's doing this – and it is she who instigates the sex – solely as a safety precaution in case they need to demonstrate their love and intimacy when applying for a deferral. It is as if she is too repressed to acknowledge her own feelings. It isn't until she's stumbling through what she wants to say to Madame that she at last says, 'We know you must get tired of it, these couples coming to you claiming to be in love. Tommy and me, we never would have come and bothered you if we weren't really sure' (p. 247).

### Key quotation

'When we had proper sex and we were really happy about it, even then, this same nagging feeling would always be there.'
(p. 235)

### Key quotation

'…if…we did find ourselves going for a deferral, it might prove a real drawback if we'd never had sex.'
(p. 234)

On page 94 Kathy observes in passing that nobody at Hailsham was 'at all kind towards any signs of gay stuff' (p. 94). Ironically there seems to be what the students refer to as an 'umbrella' (p. 94) relationship being conducted under their noses. Kathy – and the reader – learns at the end of the novel that Miss Emily and Madame have worked closely together for decades for the welfare of clones and recognition of their humanity. They are now living together, having lost Hailsham, addressing each other affectionately, and we may be expected to presume that they are a couple who love each other.

Also remember the professional love that Kathy – a good carer – applies to the donors she supports. She cares for them and looks after them in a loving way, telling the reader that she has 'developed a kind of instinct around donors' (p. 3).

# Loss

Ishiguro's narrator, Kathy, has lost everything by the end of the novel: Ruth, Tommy and Hailsham. Ruth and Tommy have both, by this point, suffered the ultimate loss and died. And soon Kathy will lose her life. All she has left, as she says on page 281, are her memories, which no one can take from her. All three characters have, in a sense, lost the opportunity of a loving relationship with the parents they never had and all chance of a normal, fulfilled life.

## Key quotation

*'It's like with my memories of Tommy and of Ruth. Once I'm able to have a quieter life, in whichever centre they send me to, I'll have Hailsham with me, safely in my head, and that'll be something no one can take away.'*
(p. 281)

Miss Emily and Madame have lost both Hailsham and their dream of making things better for student clones – along with most of their money. Even at the time of Kathy and Tommy's visit, a bedside cabinet is being sold – and lost (see 'Symbolism', on p. 69 of this guide). When Kathy loses her tape she feels bereft and lost because it was one of her few, treasured possessions and a trigger for wistful happy dreams. And the disappointed Chrissie and Rodney eventually lose each other when they embark on the donation programme.

And all this is tied up with the notion that begins as a school joke, of Norfolk as the 'lost corner' of England, and Norfolk later becomes the place where Chrissie and Rodney finally lose hope. At the end of the novel Kathy imagines everything she has lost since childhood, including Tommy, being washed up on a Norfolk beach.

## Build critical skills

In his 1850 poem 'In Memoriam', Alfred Lord Tennyson wrote: ''Tis better to have loved and lost / Than never to have loved at all.' Do you think, from the presentation of love and loss in *Never Let Me Go*, that Kazuo Ishiguro agrees with Tennyson?

## GRADE *FOCUS*

### Grade 5

To achieve Grade 5 you will need to show a clear understanding of how Ishiguro presents a theme through his use of language, form and (where appropriate) structure, supported by appropriate references to the text.

### Grade 8

To achieve this grade you will examine and evaluate the key themes of the novel, perceptively analysing the ways that Ishiguro uses language, form and structure to explore them. Comments will be supported by carefully chosen and well-integrated references to the text.

## REVIEW YOUR LEARNING

(Answers are given on p. 110.)

1  What is a theme? What use does Ishiguro make of themes?
2  Name three of the main themes of *Never Let Me Go*.
3  Give two examples of loss in the novel.
4  Why does Miss Emily find clones like Kathy and Tommy 'repulsive'?
5  Who mentions death overtly, and when?

# Target your thinking

- How does the author reveal his story to the readers? (**AO2**)
- When and where is the novel set and what effect does this have? (**AO3**)
- What language techniques does Ishiguro use and why? (**AO2**)
- How does Ishiguro use symbols? (**AO2**)
- How realistic is *Never Let Me Go* meant to be? (**AO1**, **AO2**)

You will notice from these questions that when analysing language and style the Assessment Objective with which we are most concerned is AO2. AO2 refers to the writer's methods and is usually highlighted in exam questions by the word 'how'. Language and style are of vital importance since they are the medium through which writers help to create our understanding of plot, character and themes.

## Kathy's voice

As we have seen, *Never Let Me Go* is constructed entirely as a first person narrative, with Kathy H. as the sole narrator. The voice Ishiguro creates for her is painstaking ('I want just to say a bit about our Sales', p. 41), flat, dull, repetitive, controlled and humourless. She repeats the cautious 'I don't know how it was where you were...' several times in Part One, for example. It seems as if she is trying to be honest with the reader and spell out everything that is worrying her. In fact, her real worries are concealed behind the recollection of trivia such as the 'tokens controversy' (p. 38). Even as an adult she can't see how little such small things really matter.

> **GRADE BOOSTER**
>
> What would have been gained and what would have been lost if Ishiguro had written the novel in the third person instead of the first? Showing an understanding of the effects of using the first person narrative could enhance your grade.

She is what literary critics call an 'unreliable narrator'. She is not revealing most of what Ishiguro wants us to understand is actually going on, because she herself has limited understanding of this. Beneath her earnestly detailed account of school life at Hailsham and her often troubled relationship with Ruth and Tommy, both there and at the Cottages, is a deeply frightened and lonely woman. Her friends are now all dead and she will embark on her path to the same fate in just a few months – nearly twelve years as a carer means that she knows precisely what the next (final) stage of her life will involve. But Ishiguro presents her as a narrator who never openly confronts her deepest fears and feelings and who never writes about them. The meaning of the novel is conveyed by inference rather than taking anything its narrator says as the truth about what is really happening. The reader is expected to see past Kathy and work out for him- or herself what she is *not* saying.

## Setting

We are told, on the title page preceding Part One, that the novel is set in England in the late 1990s. The alternative world that Ishiguro creates has had time to make medical and scientific discoveries after World War II and for those to be built into a social system by the time Kathy, Ruth and Tommy are born in the mid to late 1960s. It all happened 'so rapidly, there wasn't time to take stock, to ask sensible questions' (p. 257).

The novel has a number of settings. In the present – as Kathy anticipates the impending end of her service as a carer – she is often in her car. She drives all over the country, often mentioning places by name (e.g. Worcestershire, p. 5; North Wales, p. 211; Suffolk, p. 207), as she visits her donors and attends to the paperwork. Somewhere she has her own bedsit (mentioned on p. 3, p. 64 and p. 204), although we never see her in it. A bedsit is, anyway, not usually a permanent home. Through these details, Ishiguro implies that his narrator is rootless. She has no parents and Hailsham has closed down. She is constantly on the move and passing through places. This could be read as a metaphor for her transient life. She is passing through life in order to donate her organs to save other faceless people with whom she has had little or no contact.

## Part One

Part One of the novel is based mostly around Kathy's memories of Hailsham. Part Two covers the two or three years she is at the Cottages, from age 16 to about eighteen or nineteen. (She is 31 in the present and has been a carer for almost twelve years. Ishiguro doesn't tell us how long carer training takes.) Part Three comes up to the present and covers the latter stages of Kathy's caring years, when she finds both Ruth and Tommy again. All of this is recounted with frequent time shifts as Kathy seems to sort and share her memories, although Ishiguro is being very selective as she dives backward and forward across the years.

The Hailsham setting seems idyllic and the Guardians are kind and caring. The students undertake plenty of enjoyable activities, such as sport and art.

The grounds with the pavilion, pond and rhubarb patch seem, as Kathy recalls them, very pleasant. There is plenty of scope for play and friendship and the students seem, for the most part, happy – although there are undercurrents, such as the bullying that Tommy suffers. Overall, though, it is presented like the perfect boarding school – or at least that's how Kathy remembers it. Several times, though, Kathy gets irritated with Ruth for remembering it differently (p. 43, p. 187, p. 198, for example). Memories, Ishiguro is suggesting, are often shaped by the person doing the remembering.

Boarding schools have traditionally been portrayed in fiction as quite pleasant, jolly or exciting places, from Enid Blyton's St Clare's to J.K. Rowling's Hogwarts. By subverting that tradition, Ishiguro makes Hailsham's real purpose seem all the more chilling. Behind the apparent peace and perfection of Hailsham lies, of course, the real world of the donation programme (symbolised by the surrounding 'dark fringe of trees', p. 49), which Miss Emily and most of her staff carefully prevent the students from knowing or thinking too much about.

## Build critical skills

Why does Ishiguro present the students telling each other horrible and frightening stories about the woods beyond Hailsham? Consider, for example, the student who was rumoured to have been tied to a tree and mutilated (p. 50). How does this link to what actually happens to the students?

## Build critical skills

Consider why Ishiguro might have included the rumour of the ghost of an ex-student desperate to return to Hailsham. What might he have been suggesting?

### Key quotation

'for the first hour we all felt so exhilarated to be out and about ... Rodney actually let out a few whoops'
(p. 146)

Interestingly, given her constant driving about, Kathy does not know exactly where Hailsham was. It has since closed down as a school (p. 207) and its buildings are now used for something else, but it has, effectively, disappeared like a dream (p. 6). Ishiguro deliberately makes Kathy very specific and realistic about other geographical settings. The Norfolk trip is to Cromer, and Miss Emily lives with Madame in Littlehampton, for example. This serves to highlight Kathy's otherworldly complete loss of Hailsham as a physical and geographical actuality. For her it has gone, except in her memory – and she remembers it as she wants to (pp. 280–81). In contrast, the simple, almost mundane, description of the everyday activities and other locations seems to make the real purpose of the lives of Ishiguro's teenagers even more disturbing.

## Part Two

The Cottages, where Part Two is predominantly set, are scruffy (p. 115) but more adult than school. Students are left more or less to their own devices, with practical needs serviced by the visiting Keffers. The atmosphere is 'easy-going' and 'languid' (p. 117). Three chapters are given to the pivotal trip to Cromer made by Ruth, Tommy, Kathy, Chrissie and Rodney (Chapters 13–15). For students who have seen very little of the outside world, its exploration is to begin with a trip to an exciting place on a 'crisp, sunny day' (p. 146).

Ishiguro shows the students' naivety by their utter delight at a notice containing the word 'Look' with the eyes drawn inside each 'o'. Kathy is delighted by the inside of Woolworths, and all three stare at and are fascinated by the glossy interior of the office.

Cromer, however, despite its attractions proves, for Ruth, Rodney and Chrissie, to be a backdrop to disappointment. Ishiguro reflects the deflated mood when he uses pathetic fallacy, as the students wander through 'little backstreets hardly penetrated by the sun' along 'pavements so narrow we often had to shuffle along in single file' (p. 154). Rodney, no longer whooping, struggles to find his way to the office where he claims to have seen a possible for Ruth.

Chrissie and Rodney lose all hope of a deferral when they realise that the Hailsham students can tell them nothing useful. Despite a short period of optimism, Ruth loses face, and her temper, as well as the hope of finding her 'possible' (p. 164).

Ishiguro also uses this visit to suggest the perceived attitudes of a hostile public to the clones.

### Key quotation

*'Art students, that's what she thought we were. Do you think she'd have talked to us like that if she'd known what we really were?'*
(p. 164)

It is in Cromer, however, that a bond is re-established between Kathy and Tommy, who spend most of the rest of the day affectionately together and who find another copy of Kathy's tape, lost years before.

### Key quotation

*'That moment when we decided to go searching for my lost tape, it was like suddenly every cloud had blown away, and we had nothing but fun and laughter before us.'*
(p. 169)

Gradually it becomes clear that there is no real purpose in life at the Cottages. No one does any work beyond domestic chores. Even the essay that the Hailsham students had been told they must complete at this stage dwindles in importance and doesn't get done (p. 113). It's a rather tense, unreal commune – an interim post-school holding place. 'We certainly didn't think much about our lives beyond the Cottages, or about who ran them, or how they fitted into the larger world' (p. 114).

Eventually, after the Norfolk trip, Kathy recognises the futility of living at the Cottages as an adjunct to Ruth and Tommy and volunteers to start training as a carer (p. 199). That marks the beginning of the long period in which she has no contact with Ruth and Tommy.

**Key** quotation

*The surroundings of the Cottages: '…seemed to us oddly crooked, like when you draw a picture of a friend, and it's almost right but not quite, and the face on the sheet gives you the creeps.'*
(p. 116)

## Part Three

Part Three involves a lot of travelling as Kathy looks back on her (almost) twelve years as a carer and the solitude that involves. 'For the most part being a carer suited me just fine,' she says with her usual disingenuity. She then describes (pp. 203–04) just how difficult it really is, while pretending to the reader and herself that she's generally happy with it. Then Ishiguro shows us Laura's despair, through Kathy (pp. 204–06), as an insight into just what a difficult life carers endure.

Kathy's car is, effectively, part of the setting too. She never tells us any details about the car itself but stresses its value to her as a quiet place to think and reflect (pp. 113, 204). The car journeys also act as a link between places and periods in the novel, even an escape mechanism, as Kathy keeps returning from her memories to herself and the car – rather like a piece of music that regularly returns to its main melody.

**Key** quotation

*'But I do like the feeling of getting into my little car, knowing for the next couple of hours I'll have only the roads, the big grey sky and my daydreams for company.'*
(p. 204)

## Imagery

'Imagery' refers to the description of something by comparing it with pictures – images – of other things that are in some way similar. It is closely related to 'imagination', a word that comes from the same root in Latin. Imagery is an 'umbrella term' and includes similes, metaphors, personification and other forms of description. Sometimes the term 'figurative language' is used instead of 'imagery'.

Because Kathy's voice is so even and controlled – unimaginative perhaps, because she is frightened of where her imagination might take her – she uses few metaphors and similes. However, the term 'imagery' can also be used to refer to visual representation generally. Ishiguro creates striking descriptive images of, for example, Hailsham, the beached boat and the forlorn Norfolk field at the end of the novel (see 'Symbolism', on p. 69 of this guide).

The barbed wire, for example, which Ruth, Tommy and Kathy have to pass through to get to the abandoned boat (p. 218) and the double line of barbed wire between Kathy and the field (p. 281) are linked images. In both cases we see human beings prevented by a painful, obstructing barrier from reaching something open and free. You might also comment on its poignant associations with twentieth century warfare. Because it occurs more than once in the novel barbed wire becomes a symbol (of constraint and pain) as well as an image.

▲ Barbed wire is a repeated image in the novel

## Speech and dialogue within narrative voice

Because *Never Let Me Go* is a first person narrative the language we hear is all Kathy's, or is filtered through her. Ishiguro wants to make her memories seem natural – like a chatty diary – although there is little sense of who, within the novel itself, Kathy's intended readership is. Her repeated 'I don't know how it was where you were' hints vaguely that she might be 'speaking' to other carers and donors.

Kathy's narrative language is often quite informal: 'Anyway, I'm not making any big claims for myself' (p. 3), 'Now it's a bit hard to explain this' (p. 127), 'The old guy behind the counter' (p. 171), 'God knows how these things work' (p. 211). It often feels more oral than written, as if she were speaking aloud to a recording device as opposed to sitting in her bedsit with a pen and paper. Ishiguro achieves this by having Kathy use idiomatic, slightly colloquial expressions, such as 'a complete waste of space' (p. 5), 'Anyway, the point is…' (p. 65) or 'In the end, as I said' (p. 145), particularly when she's addressing the reader directly.

Kathy often begins sentences with conjunctions too, which is informal rather than grammatically conventional in a written piece. 'But now the tape machine in my car's got so dodgy, I daren't play it in that' (p. 64), for example, or 'And even at the Cottages it wasn't a topic you'd bring up casually' (p. 136). Sometimes she asks a question that she then goes on to answer: 'So what had been going on?' (p. 92).

## Build critical skills

'But then everything changed again, and that was because of the boat' (p. 211). At the start of an anecdote, Ishiguro sometimes uses a 'narrative hook' like this one, i.e. something is mentioned, its significance is implied, and then Kathy explains what happened and why it was important. What is the effect of this? Find at least one other example.

## Build critical skills

What do you learn from the language used by the five characters and the words used to express Kathy's analysis in the conversation on pages 150–53?

## Key quotation

'The odd thing about our Norfolk trip was that once we got back we hardly talked about it.' (p. 182)

When Ishiguro presents her describing incidents and conversations with others, the style becomes slightly more bookish. Look at the dialogue between Ruth, Tommy, Kathy, Chrissie and Rodney on pages 150–53, for example. Kathy tells the reader who says what, as a conventional novelist would. She also comments on the way the others react to each other so you get her views and memories of what happened at the same time.

Kathy quite often speaks in short sentences consisting mostly of single-syllable words, which makes her language seem deceptively childlike and honest: 'God knows how these things work' (p. 211), 'To be fair a lot of it might have been down to me as much as him' (p. 272). This is partly what makes her speech seem so flat and emotionless.

Kathy's private – direct to the reader – language, as we have seen, is sometimes used to indicate self-delusion. Kathy repeatedly assures the reader (and herself) that she is happy to retire from her life as a carer at the end of the year. 'Once I have a quieter life, in whichever centre they send me to', she says simply on page 281, for example. The carefully chosen language indicates that she is not allowing herself to think about the forthcoming 'drugs and the pain and the exhaustion' (p. 5) or 'the horror movie stuff' (p. 274), or at least not in relation to herself.

## Build critical skills

Find at least four examples of Kathy saying something that can't be completely true, i.e. occasions when the language Ishiguro gives her indicates she is refusing to face reality. Copy the quotations (with page numbers) as part of your note-making.

Speech and dialogue is also used as part of characterisation. Ruth, for example, often speaks sneeringly to others. 'I had to really dig it out of Sweet Boy here. Not very keen at all on letting me in on it were you, sweety gums?' she says unpleasantly on page 191 when she is speaking to Kathy about Tommy's art.

Miss Emily has a crisp manner, suitable for a headmistress. Kathy describes her 'quiet deliberate voice' (p. 39). Even under stress her speech mode is formally correct and much less casual than Kathy's, perhaps because Ishiguro wants to present her as guarded in her speech. 'Marie-Claude is correct' and 'I'm the one to whom you should be speaking', she says on page 251.

Madame is more enigmatic. 'Very well then. Come inside. Then we'll see what you want to talk about' (p. 243). Later she drops her guard and bursts out with 'Poor creatures. What did we do to you?', spoken 'barely audibly' (p. 249). As usual in this novel the language given to characters to speak is interspersed with Kathy's comments.

In the world of *Never Let Me Go*, euphemisms (gentle, evasive words or expressions for unmentionable things) are part of normal speech. Kathy uses them and so does everyone she meets. Thus clones reared to be harvested for their organs are known as 'students' long after they cease to study anything. Death is known as 'completion' and after organ removal surgery the clones are taken to 'recovery centres', in which they certainly won't recover – or will only briefly do so in preparation for the next operation.

## Symbolism

A symbol is an object that stands for an idea, feeling or point of view. Or to put it more formally, it is a tangible representation of an abstraction. For example, a national flag is a symbol of the nation that bears it. A red poppy is a symbol for the loss of life in war.

In literature, writers – of fiction, plays and poetry – sometimes introduce objects that have, or acquire, symbolic significance. An ordinary everyday thing comes to represent something bigger. Kazuo Ishiguro is such a writer and *Never Let Me Go* relies quite heavily on symbolism. Look carefully, therefore, at anything that initially *seems* to be pointless or irrelevant in the novel and work out why it's there. Consider the following examples.

### Miss Emily's bedside cabinet

When Tommy and Kathy visit Madame and, as it turns out, Miss Emily in Chapters 21 and 22, they find them in the process of selling a precious bedside cabinet. Miss Emily describes it as a 'wonderful object' and a 'beautiful object' (p. 252) and says she had it with her at Hailsham.

It seems, on the surface, like a fussy digression. But this is a very carefully crafted novel and Ishiguro allows nothing to wander into it by accident. The cabinet is a symbol of the ideals that Miss Emily has striven for and

**Build critical skills**

Ishiguro has created for his characters a universal speech mode, which keeps the truth below the surface and helps to enable most of them to deny their future deaths most of the time. How might this affect the reader?

has had to give up. It is valuable and lovely but she now has to let it go – note the link with the novel's title. Just as she once cosseted and protected her students, she now insists that George, her carer, wrap the cabinet in 'protective' padding because otherwise it might be handled roughly and hurled around the vehicle (p. 252).

## The boat

Ruth tells Kathy that she'd like to visit an abandoned fishing boat she's heard about. It is 'just sitting there, stranded in the marshes' (p. 212) not far from the road and has become a minor tourist attraction somewhere along the south coast, about an hour and half (p. 12) from Ruth's recovery centre at Dover. They visit it with Tommy, on pages 222–23. While there they discuss the graphic horror of donation, which Ruth tells Kathy she can't possibly understand fully. They can't get very close to the boat but agree that they're glad to have seen it. They finally leave in a chilly wind (p. 223).

The boat, which otherwise seems a rather odd thing to have included (they could have visited a museum or park, after all, if it was just a way to get the three of them together), symbolises the lonely future of isolated death that each of them faces. The boat can no longer catch the tide and sail away freely. It is damaged and stuck. In the same way, the students are prisoners of the donation programme with no choices and nowhere to go. They too are damaged and stuck.

## The woods around Hailsham

Hailsham is a nurturing, pleasant environment. Students have almost no contact with the outside world except a quick occasional word with the kindly men who deliver the junk for the Sales (pp. 41–42). The children feel safe and sheltered there.

> **GRADE BOOSTER**
>
> A word of warning. Symbolism is important in *Never Let Me Go*, but don't get so bogged down trying to analyse it that you look for and try to contrive symbolic significance in everything in the novel. The car that Rodney borrows and drives to Norfolk (p. 144) is probably just a car, for example. And it's reasonable to assume that the ducks, bulrushes and pond weed on the Hailsham pond (p. 25) can also be taken at face value.

Beyond Hailsham House, with its tranquil fields and lake, are woods: 'a dark fringe of trees' (p. 49). These are presented as a fairly obvious symbol of the menacing, threatening outside world. Kathy says: 'I certainly wasn't the only one to feel their presence day and night. When it got bad, it was like they cast a shadow over the whole of Hailsham; all you had to do was turn your head or move towards a window and there they'd be' (pp. 49–50).

## Build critical skills

The students punish Marge K. for 'embarrassing' them by forcing her to look out at the woods from the window: 'At first she kept her eyes screwed shut, but we twisted her arms and forced open her eyelids until she saw the distant outline against the moonlit sky, and that was enough to ensure for her a sobbing night of terror' (pp. 50–51). What does this quotation reveal about Kathy and the other students and about their attitudes to the outside world?

The Hailsham children, over time, have created their own myths and horror stories about the dangers of the world outside the grounds, which the guardians tell them are nonsense (p. 50). Older students tell them that they will one day be told the truth.

## Norfolk

The East Anglian county of Norfolk is a symbol of loss on several levels in *Never Let Me Go*.

Hailsham children call Norfolk the 'lost corner of England' because Miss Emily has no illustration of it for her geography lessons (pp. 65–67). At the end of the novel Kathy stands, on a bleak, windy day, gazing through rubbish-strewn barbed wire and trees at the Norfolk landscape, and reflects on her losses, consciously aware of the symbolism: 'This was Norfolk after all' (p. 282).

▼ What does Norfolk represent for Kathy, Ruth and Tommy?

Norfolk

## Build critical skills

What might be the symbolic significance of the following?
● Tommy's animals
● the clown with the balloons (p. 215)
● barbed wire (p. 218)
● Ruth's pencil case (p. 56)
● Kathy's lost (and replaced) tape.

# Realism

As you work on *Never Let Me Go* you, as the reader, must decide just how realistic (or not) Ishiguro intends it to be and whether or not it matters. There is no right or wrong answer to the realism question but it is something you need to think about in order to make up your own mind.

On the surface of the novel the action seems to take place in a world very much like our own – or at least as it was in the period leading up to the late 1990s. During the Norfolk trip, for example, the students have lunch in a very ordinary café and go shopping in Woolworths (a ubiquitous chain of high street stores that has since closed). The 31-year-old Kathy uses motorway service stations and buys lamps for her bedsit.

On the other hand, there are many things in *Never Let Me Go* that don't add up realistically and which give much of the novel an otherworldly atmosphere. Consider, for example, the following unanswered questions.

- Why is there never any traffic on the roads that Kathy drives on constantly? And does she never go through a town? She seems always to be on lonely, rural roads thinking quiet reflective thoughts. Perhaps this links to the somewhat dream-like quality of the narrative.

- The donation programme and the clone-rearing initiative would cost an unimaginable amount of money. How is it being paid for? The only real glimpse of the outside world we get in the novel is at Cromer, where life seems to be recognisably ordinary. There is no indication of a way of life that would fund this national expenditure.

- If the students are as frightened of the future as Ishiguro makes it clear they are, then why do they not go into hiding or run away to another country? They are free to do as they wish while they're at the Cottages, after all; for example Rodney has learned to drive, and he borrows a car and takes four other people to Cromer for the day.

- Where does the students' money come from while they're at the Cottages? They make purchases in Cromer so they must get money from somewhere.

The answers to these and other similar questions raised by *Never Let Me Go* may be that the world presented in the novel does not function quite like the real world. It is not meant to be realistic or totally plausible. Why do you think Ishiguro has chosen to write in this way? You might look back at the material under 'Death' on pages 51–53 of this guide for one possible explanation.

**GRADE *FOCUS***

**Grade 5**

To achieve Grade 5 you will need to show clear understanding of how Ishiguro selects language, form and structure to convey his ideas, supported by appropriate textual references.

**Grade 8**

To achieve this grade you will explore and analyse the methods that Ishiguro uses to create effects for the reader, supported by carefully chosen and well-integrated references to the text.

## REVIEW YOUR LEARNING

(Answers are given on pp. 110–111.)

1   Where and when does Ishiguro set *Never Let Me Go*?

2   Why does Ishiguro have Kathy speak informally to the reader?

3   Give two examples of lack of realism in *Never Let Me Go*.

4   How does Ishiguro make the outside world seem threatening for the Hailsham students?

5   What makes Kathy an unreliable narrator?

6   How does Ishiguro make Kathy's speaking/writing style seem flat?

7   What does the beached boat symbolise?

8   What does Miss Emily's bedside cabinet represent?

# Target your thinking

- What sorts of questions will you have to answer in the exam?
- What is the best way to plan your answer?
- How can you improve your grade?
- What do you have to do to achieve the highest grade?

*Never Let Me Go* is a 'closed book' text for all the examination boards that set it. This means you are not allowed to take the novel into the exam with you. Different examination boards will test you in different ways so you need to know on which paper *Never Let Me Go* will appear so that you can be well prepared on the day of the exam.

| Exam board | AQA | WJEC Eduqas | OCR |
|---|---|---|---|
| Paper and section | Paper 2: Modern texts and poetry; Section A: Modern prose or drama | Component 2 Section A: Post-1914 prose/drama | Paper 1 Modern and literary heritage texts; Section A: Exploring modern and heritage literary texts |
| Type of question | Essay with two bullet points to guide | Extract-based | Part a) Comparison of a short extract from *Never Let Me Go* with a modern, same-genre unseen extract; Part b) A related essay question on *Never Let Me Go* |
| Closed book? | Yes | Yes | Yes |
| Choice of question? | Yes | No | No |
| Paper and section length | Paper 2 = 2 hours 15 minutes Section A = approx. 45 minutes | Component 2 = 2 hours 30 minutes Section A = approx. 50 minutes | Paper 1 = 2 hours Section A: Part a) = 45 minutes; Part b) = 30 minutes |
| % of whole grade | 20% | 20% | 25% |
| AOs assessed | AO1, AO2, AO3, AO4 | AO1, AO2, AO4 | AO1, AO2, AO3 |
| Is AO4 assessed in this section? | Yes | Yes | No |

# Tackling the tasks

Remember:

- No two answers, even if they score the same mark, will contain exactly the same material.
- You can answer a question in more than one way and still score high marks.
- All your points must be supported by evidence (quotations or reference to events) from the novel.
- You must do more than retell the story: your job is to demonstrate your knowledge and understanding by commenting on the novel.
- The examiner is interested in your response to *Never Let Me Go* and what you think about it.

There are two main sorts of question that you are likely to be asked: character-focused and theme-focused. Here are some examples.

An example character-based exam-style question for AQA would be:

> Explore some of the ways in which Ishiguro presents Kathy's friends Ruth and Tommy and how he makes them into interesting, believable characters.
>
> Write about:
>
> - how Ishiguro presents Ruth and Tommy.
> - how he makes them interesting and believable.

An example theme-based exam-style question for AQA would be:

> How does Ishiguro explore the theme of friendship in *Never Let Me Go*?
>
> Write about:
>
> - how Ishiguro presents friendship in the novel.
> - how friendship develops between the characters.

If you are entered for the exam with WJEC Eduqas, you will need to respond to a short extract printed on the paper and – most importantly – also write about the issues raised in the passage as they occur throughout the novel.

An example extract-based exam-style question for WJEC Eduqas would be:

You should use the extract below and your knowledge of the novel as a whole to answer this question.

Write about Ishiguro's presentation of the relationship between Kathy and Ruth.

In your response you should:

- refer to the extract and to the novel as a whole
- show your understanding of characters, relationships and events in the novel.

Then at one point a girl called Midge A. came over to where we were and said to Ruth in a perfectly friendly way:

'Where's your pencil case? It's so luscious.'

Ruth tensed and glanced quickly around to see who was present. It was our usual gang with perhaps a couple of outsiders lurking nearby. I hadn't mentioned to a soul anything about the Sales Register business, but I suppose Ruth wasn't to know that. Her voice was softer than usual when she replied to Midge.

'I haven't got it here. I keep it in my collection chest.'

'It's so luscious. Where did you get it?

Midge was quizzing her completely innocently, that was now obvious. But almost all of us who'd been in Room 5 the time Ruth had first brought out the pencil case were here now, looking on and I saw Ruth hesitate. It was only later when I replayed it all, that I appreciated how perfectly shaped a chance it was for me. At the time I didn't really think. I just came in before Midge or anyone else had the chance to notice that Ruth was in a curious quandary.

'We can't say where it came from.'

Ruth, Midge, the rest of them, they all looked at me, maybe a little surprised. But I kept my cool and went on, addressing only Midge.

'There are some very good reasons why we can't tell you where it came from.'

Midge shrugged. 'So it's a mystery.'

'A *big* mystery,' I said, then gave her a smile to show her I wasn't being nasty to her.

The others were nodding to back me up, though Ruth herself had on a vague expression, like she'd suddenly become preoccupied with something else entirely. Midge shrugged again, and as far as I remember that was the end of it. Either she walked off, or else started talking about something different.

Now for much the same reasons I'd not been able to talk openly to Ruth about what I'd done to her over the Sales Register business, she of course, wasn't able to thank me for the way I'd intervened with Midge.

**(pp. 62–63)**

# Planning your answers

Always work out what the question is asking you to do and make a plan before you begin. In an exam when you are under time pressure, you will have to do this quickly. You may wish to underline key words in the question, such as 'how' to remind you to write about the author's methods, and any other words that you feel will help you focus on answering the question. Below is an example of an exam-style question that has been annotated in this way:

Explore some of the ways in which Ishiguro presents Kathy's friends Ruth and Tommy and how he makes them into interesting, believable characters.

Write about:

- how Ishiguro presents Ruth and Tommy.
- how he makes them interesting and believable.

Now devise an essay plan – even two or three minutes spent making a plan will pay off. Your answer will be better thought out and better shaped, and you are less likely to miss out important points if you have noted them in your plan.

Experiment with different sorts of plan and decide what works for you. Some people are visual learners and prefer diagrammatic plans. This usually means putting the key idea in a circle in the middle of the page and adding points for inclusion, linked to the key idea, around the outside. Alternatively, you could make a list and number the points.

You are unlikely to be able to make more than five or six main points in the body of your answer in the time available to you in the exam. Always plan also to 'frame' your answer with a meaningful introduction and a conclusion.

Try to plan your time carefully so that you always complete your answer.

**GRADE** *BOOSTER*

If you misjudge the time in your exam and do not finish, hand in your plan so that the examiner can see your intentions. It could mean an extra mark or two – perhaps enough to push your work into the next grade.

# Essay openings

You will gain no marks for repeating the question in your opening sentence or paragraph. Instead, your introduction might:

- say how you are going to tackle the question
- interpret the question (say what you think it means)
- comment on something that is in the question
- make some general introductory remarks that focus clearly on the question and begin to meet the AOs.

The examiner's aim is to seek out the mark-scoring parts of your essay. You *will* score marks for making informed analytical comments. Your time is limited – do not waste it writing anything else.

Below are four possible introductions for an essay answering the following AQA exam-style question. Which do you consider most effective and why?

> Examine the ways in which Ishiguro develops the changing relationship between Kathy and Tommy during the course of the novel.
>
> Write about:
>
> - how Ishiguro presents Kathy and Tommy's relationship.
> - how the relationship between them changes.

- At the beginning of the novel Ishiguro has Kathy, 31, remembering how she supported Tommy at Hailsham when she tried to understand him during his part-disturbing, part-comical rages. By the end of the novel Ishiguro has shown her falling in love with Tommy, having her hopes of future time together dashed and finally losing him to death.

- Never Let Me Go is, in some ways, a novel about lack of change and that's what Ishiguro invites us to think about. The students are powerless to change their own futures, but Tommy and Kathy have seen their relationship change from a loving childish friendship to a full-blown love affair. In Ishiguro's disturbing created world, the change in them is counterpointed against the inflexibility of the system they live in.

- Ishiguro develops the changing relationship between Tommy and Kathy through several incidents. These include the Norfolk trip, Kathy's realisation at the Cottages that she has to leave Tommy and Ruth to get on with being a couple, Kathy's decision to become Tommy's carer, their visit to Miss Emily, and Tommy finally sending Kathy away.

- At first Kathy is puzzled by Tommy and his tantrums but feels instinctively sympathetic when the others are bullying or laughing at him. Ishiguro soon makes things happen to develop this sympathy.

# Essay endings

You will get no extra marks for repeating in your conclusion something that you have said already. Instead, in your conclusion you might:

- summarise your arguments and draw them together in a new way
- make a new but linked point that you have deliberately held back for the ending
- try to be 'punchy' so that there is the sense of an essay that has been finished, rather than just tailing off.

Below are two possible conclusions for the same AQA exam-style essay title used above. Which do you think is the most effective and why?

- At the very end of the novel Ishiguro has Kathy standing at a remote spot in Norfolk and imagining that 'everything I'd ever lost since my childhood had washed up'. This includes Tommy, whom she imagines walking up the field towards her. The last paragraph of Never Let Me Go indicates clearly that Ishiguro wants the reader to know that the relationship between Kathy and Tommy is complete in every sense. It began 25 years earlier, changed and is now finally finished. The term 'completion' is indeed double-edged.

- I believe, and have tried to show, that Ishiguro presents the relationship between Kathy and Tommy as constantly changing as they follow, without choice, the 'course that has been set' for their lives. The relationship between Kathy and Tommy is the central one in the novel, which is why their final loss of each other is so moving.

# Using evidence in essays

Just as scientists provide evidence to back up their theories, you need to provide evidence to back up the points in your essay. All the evidence you require lies between the covers of *Never Let Me Go*.

There are two ways of providing evidence from the novel.

## Quotation of exact words written in the novel

This means you look for short phrases that illustrate your point and weave them into your sentences. Always remember to include quotation marks. You should not need to quote more than one sentence at a time. Aim to work at least eight direct quotations or close textual references into an exam essay. Structure your sentences like the following examples:

- Kathy claims, not always convincingly, to be able to deal with life as a carer, with 'the long hours, the travelling, the broken sleep.'
- Miss Emily is presented as an unflappable woman who can thrust 'her pointer around without the least self-consciousness' during sex education lessons.
- Nobody, 'not the whitecoats, not the carers – and usually not the donors', in *Never Let Me Go* wants to think about the reality of the future, which is why Kathy is surprised and very hurt by Tommy sending her away before his fourth donation.

## Close reference to incidents in the novel without quoting directly

Consider the examples of close referencing below:

- Kathy's detailed description of the 'tokens controversy' demonstrates the insularity of protective Hailsham. It also makes it clear that these children get very excited about being allowed to own other people's cast-off possessions. It reinforces the poignancy of their situation.
- On the occasion when Kathy meets Ruth and Tommy near an old church not far from the Cottages, yet again Ishiguro shows the rising tensions between the three of them. Ruth contemptuously dismisses Tommy's drawings and Kathy, years later, wishes she'd defended him.
- Miss Lucy's outburst reveals that she believes the Hailsham students should be told the truth and not allowed to look forward to things, such as careers, that they will never have. As such, Ishiguro uses her views to contrast with Miss Emily's views.

> **GRADE** *BOOSTER*
>
> The more widely you read, the better your vocabulary and command of English is likely to be. Most people soak up good writing habits unconsciously from reading. So, as well as studying your set texts, read as much other fiction as you can. Read biographies, newspapers and websites, too. This could help you to express yourself more fluently in essays.

## Essay writing tips

Six 'do' tips:

- Focus clearly on the exam question, ensuring you answer all parts of it.
- Make a brief plan of five or six key points before you start.

- Be selective about what you choose to write about, focusing on providing depth and detail.
- Support your points with evidence from the novel.
- Spell and punctuate accurately – especially key terms and the names of characters or places in the novel.
- Manage your time carefully – leave yourself a few minutes at the end to check your work.

...And six 'don'ts':

- Don't retell the story.
- Don't waste your time writing out long quotations that are not grafted tightly to your arguments.
- Don't begin sentences or paragraphs with phrases like: 'The above quotation shows...'
- Don't try to write everything you know about *Never Let Me Go*.
- Don't confuse Ishiguro (the author) with Kathy (his fictional narrator).
- Don't misspell words such as *Ishiguro*, *Hailsham*, *donor* and *Norfolk*. Remember to address AO4.

## REVIEW YOUR LEARNING

(Answers are given on p. 111.)

1 On which paper is your *Never Let Me Go* question?
2 Can you take your copy of the novel into the exam?
3 Will you have a choice of question?
4 How long do you have to answer the question?
5 What advice would you give to another student about using quotations?
6 Will you be assessed on spelling, punctuation and grammar in your response to *Never Let Me Go*?
7 Why is it important to plan your answer?
8 What should you do if you finish ahead of time?

All GCSE examinations are pinned to very specific areas of learning that the examiners want to be sure candidates have mastered. These are known as Assessment Objectives (AOs).

Think of AOs as dartboard-like targets or like the ones on a shooting range. The examiner is watching the target. You aim for it. You get marks if you hit it but not if you don't – and, in general, the more direct your hit, the more marks you are likely to get.

# What are the AOs and what do they mean?

This is the definition of the AOs used by all four boards:

---

**AO1** Read, understand and respond to texts. Students should be able to:
- maintain a critical style and develop an informed personal response
- use textual references, including quotations, to support and illustrate interpretations.

**AO2** Analyse the language, form and structure used by a writer to create meanings and effects, using relevant subject terminology where appropriate.

**AO3** Show understanding of the relationship between texts and the contexts in which they were written.

**AO4** Use a range of vocabulary and sentence structures for clarity, purpose and effect, with accurate spelling and punctuation.

---

# What skills do you need to show?

So, what do these rather complicated AO statements actually mean, and what are examiners really looking for?

---

**AO1** Read, understand and respond to texts. Students should be able to:
- maintain a critical style and develop an informed personal response
- use textual references, including quotations, to support and illustrate interpretations.

---

For AO1, you are required to show that you have read the novel carefully and thought about it from a number of angles. At its most basic level this Assessment Objective is about having a good grasp of what the text is about and being able to express an opinion about it in relation to the question. If, for example, you were to say 'The novel is about an apprehensive 31-year-old coming to terms with loss', you would be beginning to address AO1 because the words 'apprehensive' and 'loss' indicate that you have made a personal judgement informed by your reading of the novel.

In order to formulate a detailed informed personal response you need to have travelled in your mind to Hailsham and the other places Kathy mentions, to have considered how she, Ruth, Tommy, Miss Emily and Madame must have felt, and thought carefully about why. That is imaginative reading. But of course to meet this AO you also have to express it critically.

Remember – and this is the second part of AO1 – that every point (or 'interpretation') you make must be supported with relevant 'textual references'. That means that you use brief quotations or refer to incidents in the text as evidence to support what you say.

> **AO2**  Analyse the language, form and structure used by a writer to create meanings and effects, using relevant subject terminology where appropriate.

This AO requires you to show that you understand not just *what* Kazuo Ishiguro has written in *Never Let Me Go* but also *how* he has used his writer's tools. Like all authors, Ishiguro has used language very precisely for specific purposes and he has chosen to shape his novel to tell his story in a particular way. The novel's 'language, form and structure' covers things such as:

- Ishiguro's use of an adult narrator looking back on her childhood (in Part One) and therefore able to use adult language.
- His use of a rather strange emotionless style to suggest the suppression of real feelings. Note that Kathy never says she loves Tommy, either to him or to the reader, although she clearly does.
- His use of flashbacks and digressions.
- His requirement that the reader make inferences by reading 'between the lines'. Ishiguro is not an author who spells everything out explicitly.

Using 'relevant subject terminology where appropriate' could involve referring to Ishiguro's extensive use of symbolism and thematic imagery (such as the barbed wire or the menacing woods), his use of a first person narrator, and terms such as 'theme', 'narrative method' and many more. You must remember, however, that it is not enough simply to identify these features. You must explain the effects they create for the reader. There are, for example, very few marks for saying 'Ishiguro uses many symbols' or 'When he shows Miss Emily selling a bedside cabinet that she values, he is using a symbol' without going on to explain their effects.

One way of making sure that you write 'critically' is not to lose sight of the novel being something that Ishiguro has created. Make statements beginning, for instance:

- *Kazuo Ishiguro makes us aware…*
- *Ishiguro presents…*
- *The author makes it clear that…*
- *Ishiguro makes Kathy say…*
- *Ishiguro implies through Kathy…*
- *Ishiguro wants to show the reader that…*

Critical reading and writing involves awareness of why Ishiguro makes the decisions that he does. Why, for instance, does he make Kathy the narrator, and not Ruth or Miss Emily? Would it have been a better or worse novel if he had told the story differently? What use does he make of 'lesser characters', such as Chrissie and Rodney or Madame? Some answers to these questions are suggested in earlier sections of this guide.

| **AO3** Show understanding of the relationship between texts and the contexts in which they were written. |
| --- |

This AO is not applicable to the WJEC Eduqas question on *Never Let Me Go*.

AO3 involves:

- Showing that you understand the context in which the novel was written and is set, the tradition in which it was written, and how it might compare with other texts.
- Exploring the situation the novel presents in comparison with other situations at other times and in other places. In the case of *Never Let Me Go* this includes the ideas that underpin the novel, such as the questions Ishiguro asks about morality, society and what makes us human. This is discussed in detail in the 'Context' section of this guide (p. 10).

Of course, the main three aspects of context – social, cultural and historical – are closely related to each other and there is a lot of overlap. Bear the context in mind as you read, study and write about *Never Let Me Go*. You cannot make sense of the novel without it. When it comes to including references to context in your exam responses, be sure they are always relevant to the question and are made with close reference to the novel itself.

Be aware, though, that the number of marks allocated to AO3 is fewer than those for AO1 and AO2 in most cases. Make sure you meet AO3 but remember that AO1 and AO2 carry more marks.

> **AO4**  Use a range of vocabulary and sentence structures for clarity, purpose and effect, with accurate spelling and punctuation.

This AO is sometimes referred to as 'SPaG' (spelling, punctuation and grammar). Note that it is not applicable to the OCR question on *Never Let Me Go*.

This AO is self-explanatory. You will get a few extra marks on papers set by WJEC Eduqas and AQA if you use English appropriately and accurately with a high standard of spelling and punctuation. The best policy is to be as good at this as you can in *all* your GCSE papers, whether or not it is being specifically assessed. Be particularly careful with the spelling of proper nouns, such as *Marie-Claude, Littlehampton, Kingsfield* and so on. And make sure you can spell potentially tricky words that you will almost certainly need in your answer: *deferral, suppression, awkwardness, atmosphere, exhaustion*, for example.

Try to keep your sentences crisp and remember to end them with full stops rather than an indiscriminate scattering of commas. Exclamation marks are best avoided completely except when you're quoting direct speech. This AO is worth 2.5 per cent of the marks for AQA and WJEC Eduqas; this may not sound much but it could be the difference between your achieving one grade and the next.

## REVIEW YOUR LEARNING

(Answers are given on pp. 111–112.)

1  What does AO1 assess?
2  What sort of material do you need to cover in order to successfully address AO2?
3  What do you understand by the term 'AO3'?
4  What is SPaG?
5  Which exam board specification are you following and what AOs should you be focusing on?

# Question 1: theme-based

The exam-style question below is typical of an AQA theme-based question (and of an OCR-style second task, although OCR doesn't provide guidance bullet points).

> How does Ishiguro present loss in *Never Let Me Go*?
>
> Write about:
>
> - how Ishiguro uses different characters to present ideas about loss.
> - how Ishiguro presents these ideas by the way he writes.

You will see below extracts from exam responses by two students who are working at different levels. You should be able to see how Student Y develops the material further than Student X to achieve a higher grade.

To address the first bullet point Student X, who is working towards a Grade 5, begins like this:

**1** There are no marks for an opening sentence like this, which simply repeats the words of the question.

This essay is about how Kazuo Ishiguro presents loss in Never Let Me Go. Kathy, Ruth and Tommy, the three main characters in Never Let Me Go, all suffer losses because the whole novel is about loss. All three students have no choice but to give (lose) their organs — which sooner or later means giving (losing) their lives. Ishiguro makes this seem even more sinister by making up a world in which nobody speaks openly and euphemisms are used. They 'complete' rather than die and they 'give donations' rather than having their organs taken whether they like it or not.

**2** Beginning to address AO1 by showing understanding of the text and commenting on the author's technique (AO2).

Kathy, the narrator, has worked for nearly twelve years as a carer. She is about to lose the life she knows and become an organ donor. In plain language, that means being harvested for spare parts for other people, although Ishiguro never has her saying this in so many words. Instead, as her narrative moves backwards and forwards in time, she doesn't think about the 'horror movie stuff' and looks forward to having a rest and not having to drive about all the time.

**3** Clear awareness of the writer.

**4** Well-embedded quotation, appropriately used.

Student Y, who is likely to achieve a Grade 8, begins like this:

At the end of the novel Kathy, the narrator, returns to Norfolk and contemplates, within the context of the loss of Tommy, the rubbish and debris caught on the fence: 'I half-closed my eyes and imagined this was the spot where everything I'd lost through my childhood had washed up…'

**1** Confident opening statement, appropriately supported by a quotation. Candidate immediately begins to address the question.

This is a very moving part of the novel. Ishiguro uses the image of the barbed wire fence to evoke Kathy's pain because of the sharpness of the barbs. Perhaps it also has echoes of disturbing images of warfare too, all of which is unnerving for the reader.

**2** Addresses AO2 with some exploration and analysis of Ishiguro's methods, such as symbolism, and the effects on the reader.

**3** Identifies Ishiguro's use of pathetic fallacy, making a convincing point.

Ishiguro also uses pathetic fallacy, as the desolate landscape of 'acres of ploughed earth' and the strength of the wind reflects the desolation and loneliness of Kathy's mood. The tears stream down her cheeks in the realisation that she has lost everything. Although previously it seemed as if she was rather unemotional in her reactions to loss, especially when compared to Tommy, I felt deep sympathy for her at this point.

She comments that no one can take her memories from her, but the reader knows that soon they will take her organs and she will lose life itself.

As Ishiguro uses Kathy as a first person narrator, the reader feels very close to her, as we have been with her since her childhood, and so the prospect of the loss of her life is devastating for the reader. Ishiguro thus concludes a novel in which loss has been a key theme.

**4** Analyses Ishiguro's use of first person narrative as part of an informed personal response.

Almost everyone in Never Let Me Go suffers devastating loss and learns to cope with it in different ways. The children all lose idyllic Hailsham when they reach the age of 16. They clearly fear this loss. Ishiguro suggests this through the rumours of the ghost child who hangs around the grounds pleading to be let in. After becoming a carer, Kathy doesn't even know exactly where Hailsham is any more as she drives around the country daydreaming about it. It is therefore almost as if it is lost in an even more significant way, as if it has ceased to exist and has therefore achieved mythical status. Ruth loses Tommy as a partner when they leave the Cottages. Kathy loses touch with both Ruth and Tommy for nearly ten years, during which time she has to be as detached as she can about the donors she works with. Each one is a loss when they 'complete', however, as even Kathy admits that she feels 'demoralised' for a while afterwards. Tommy and Kathy lose each other when they realise there is no hope for a future together. Ishiguro suggests that Tommy faces the loss of his life bravely as he doesn't want Kathy near him for 'this last bit', as Ishiguro has him euphemistically refer to his impending death.

5 Concludes with reference to the idea of the use of euphemism, an idea that is developed later in the response.

Student X continues:

Along the way Kathy has lost her beloved Judy Bridgewater tape, which she used to listen to while she dreamed about the future that really, as a clone, she would never have. And when she reaches the age of 16 she leaves cosy, nest-like Hailsham and loses it — later when she's working as a carer, and Hailsham has closed down, she doesn't even know where it is or was. After a year or two in the Cottages, Ishiguro shows her going off to begin her training as a carer, when she loses contact with Ruth and Tommy. Then, when she eventually meets Ruth and Tommy again and becomes carer to them both, her sexual relationship with Tommy doesn't last long because after the visit to Madame and Miss Emily in Littlehampton they lose all hope of a deferral.

1 Two examples of loss in the novel mentioned but points could be developed further.

2 Two further examples, which need a critical comment about how Ishiguro is developing his theme in order for the candidate to address AO2 fully.

At the very end of the novel, when Tommy is dead, Ishiguro uses symbolism when he shows Kathy going to Norfolk — 'the lost corner of England' — and thinking about everything she has lost. 'I lost Ruth, then I lost Tommy... I suppose I

**3** Identifies the writer's technique but lacks explanation of effects.

> lost Hailsham too,' she says. Ishiguro then shows her weeping a little, in a remote part of Norfolk, among rubbish caught on barbed wire and tree branches: 'the spot where everything I'd lost since my childhood had washed up.'

Student Y continues:

**1** Perceptive understanding of how contexts shape texts related to loss.

> Even Miss Emily and Madame have lost everything they have worked for now that Hailsham has been closed and they are left in financial difficulties. Ishiguro depicts these two women battling against a system that leaves them powerless. This is partly, we infer, to suggest that they cannot hold back the tide either of medical science or of impending death for everyone. The novel is the product of an era in which, in real life, ethically questionable medical breakthroughs (such as transplants, IVF and genetic modification) take place all the time, and perhaps Ishiguro is questioning whether we as humans might lose something if science is allowed to progress unchecked.
>
> It is also partly a way of characterising Miss Emily as superficially kind but at another level she and Madame accept the inevitability of loss in all its forms and are contrasted by Ishiguro with Miss Lucy, who is clearly disturbed by the idea of the loss of organs and of life. This is where, in my view, the novel becomes really interesting. She attempts to get the students to face up to what they have been 'told and not told'. Perhaps Ishiguro is exploring our own attitudes to death here. After all, we all know we are going to die one day, but most of the time we shut out that knowledge. Otherwise, we might really question what the point of life is. The losses continue to permeate Ishiguro's imaginary world. All 'students' will, without doubt, lose their organs and their lives while they are still, mostly, in their twenties, and many will respond with anger like Ruth or with resignation like Kathy.

**2** Thoughtful and insightful analysis of possible deeper meaning.

When discussing loss, Ishiguro presents Kathy's voice as very understated, even when she is describing 'horror movie stuff', such as 'her' donors not getting 'agitated' as they go into fourth donation. What actually lies behind the carefully placed euphemisms is that she manages to calm the terror of young people going to a certain death on an operating table. Ishiguro leads us to deduce that Kathy, expert at suppressing her own fear of the future, has lost the ability to yearn, grieve and reason in the way that non-cloned, non-institutionalised human beings do. Only at the very end of the novel does she, briefly, succumb and weep – but even then still in a controlled way.

**3 Continued critical analysis of both AO1 and AO2.**

Kathy's Judy Bridgewater tape, with its 'Never let me go' track, symbolises love, motherhood and all the things that a young girl would be looking forward to in real life, all of which are lost to the clones. Then the tape is lost – taken from her, perhaps by Ruth or Madame – the reader doesn't know what happens to it any more than Kathy does. Ishiguro poses more questions than he answers in this novel.

Student X concludes:

Tommy, Ruth, Miss Emily and Madame all lose too as Ishiguro runs the loss theme through almost everything that happens in Never Let Me Go. Tommy, for example, loses first Ruth, then Kathy, then hope, and then his life. Ruth meanwhile has 'completed' at second donation, having had a difficult first donation. Ishiguro wants us to think about how everyone loses everything eventually, both in the novel and in real life. No matter what, everyone has to die. That is one of the themes of Never Let Me Go.

When Kathy and Tommy visit Madame they find that she and Miss Emily live together, having long worked as a team to develop a 'more humane and

**1 Clumsy expression: 'develops the theme of loss' would be better.**

**2 Offers some foregrounding of author.**

**3 Displays an engaged response to meanings.**

**4** Sense of context is thin in this essay, which therefore fails to meet AO3 adequately. More comments on Ishiguro's underlying ideas would probably have raised the grade.

better way of doing things.' Ishiguro is here asking the reader to think about all the medical discoveries that have taken place in real life in the last fifty years. Some of them lead to difficult decisions about right and wrong. Miss Emily and Madame have now lost most of what they had and valued. Hailsham has gone, leaving the two women short of money. And they are still losing possessions – while Kathy and Tommy are there they are in the process of selling a bedside cabinet. It's a symbol of Hailsham and what Miss Emily has lost.

**5** Shows some understanding of a language technique.

I believe and have tried to show that loss is a major theme in Never Let Me Go – perhaps the most important one in the novel. That is why Ishiguro has woven experience of loss at all levels into most of his characters.

This is a generally coherent and engaged response, which just meets the AOs for Grade 5, although it would benefit from a more detailed approach to the writer's methods and effects.

Student Y concludes:

One of the most devastating losses in the novel is the description of the final separation of Kathy and Tommy and the bleak poignancy with which Ishiguro presents it. The author never has Kathy admit, even to herself, that she loves Tommy – only that they began having sex (at her instigation) and that they spent a lot of time together. Ishiguro's storytelling ensures that Kathy's love is implicit in her keenness to find Madame to ask how to apply for a deferral. When their hopes are dashed Tommy reacts with extreme emotion, reminiscent of his childhood tantrums, and in this incident Ishiguro shows the depth of his anger, as well as its futility because they now have to accept the loss of their future. Tommy begins to put distance between them. He knows that he has to face his impending death, 'this last bit', alone or with a detached carer. He feels he cannot cope with having Kathy near him. Perhaps Ishiguro

**1** Shows a continued focus on the theme of loss.

**2** Offers subtle comment on Ishiguro's method.

is showing us that reactions to loss are very varied and sometimes unpredictable too. ◄───

The way Ishiguro uses Miss Emily and Madame at the end is also interesting. They too are suffering loss. They have given their lives to Hailsham as an ideal – a thing of beauty and a certain amount of innocence alongside, and in contrast to, the ugliness of the donation programme. Now it has gone. Their idealism is no longer acceptable and they've even lost money, presumably because Hailsham was, at one level, their own business. Now Miss Emily has lost the use of part of her body and is described as 'frail and contorted'; she is clearly a broken woman mentally – which is perhaps symbolised by her use of a wheelchair. And she is, when Kathy and Tommy visit, in the process of selling a treasured bedside cabinet, a symbol of art, culture and beauty, which she had at Hailsham. The implication is that it also has sentimental value and associations with gentleness and comfort – which are about to be lost.

Never Let Me Go questions what it really means to be human in an era when ever fewer people in developed countries have religious belief to sustain them through life's hardest questions. All human beings suffer loss, which is why it is threaded through this novel. This helps to make sense of Ishiguro's inclusion of tiny incidents such as Kathy's loss of faith in Ruth, when the latter turned out not be able to play chess, all the way to Kathy's devastating vision of a Norfolk shoreline on which 'everything I'd ever lost from my childhood had washed up.'

Overall, this Grade 8 essay is a confident and competent response, which addresses all four AOs at this level. It is elegantly written and sustains a strong focus on loss throughout.

# Question 2: extract-based

The question below is typical of a WJEC Eduqas extract-based question.

> You should use the extract below and your knowledge of the novel as a whole to answer this question.
>
> Write about fear of the future and the way it is presented in *Never Let Me Go*.
>
> In your response you should:
> - refer to the extract and the novel as a whole
> - show your understanding of characters and events in the novel.

'When Rodney and I, we were up in Wales,' she said. 'The same time we heard about this girl in the clothes shop. We heard something else, something about Hailsham students. What they were saying was that some Hailsham students in the past, in special circumstances, had managed to get a deferral. That this was something you could do if you were a Hailsham student. You could ask for your donations to be put back by three, even four years. It wasn't easy, but just sometimes they'd let you do it. So long as you could convince them. So long as you *qualified*.'

Chrissie paused and looked at each of us, maybe for dramatic effect, maybe to check us for signs of recognition. Tommy and I probably had puzzled looks. Ruth had on one of her faces where you couldn't tell what was going on.

'What they said,' Chrissie continued, 'was that if you were a boy and a girl, and you were in love with each other, really properly in love and if you could show it, then the people who run Hailsham, they sorted it out for you. They sorted it out so you could have a few years together before you began your donations.'

There was now a strange atmosphere round the table, a kind of tingle going round.

'When we were in Wales,' Chrissie went on, 'the students at the White Mansion. They'd heard of this Hailsham couple, the guy had only a few weeks left before he became a carer. And they went to see someone and got everything put back three years. They were allowed to go on living there together, up at the White Mansion, three years straight, didn't have to go on with their training or anything. Three years just to themselves, because they could prove themselves properly in love.'

> It was at this point I noticed Ruth nodding with a lot of authority. Chrissie and Rodney noticed too and for a few minutes they watched her like they were hypnotised. And I had a kind of vision of Chrissie and Rodney back at the Cottages, in the months leading up to this moment, probing and prodding this subject between them. I could see them bringing it up, at first very tentatively, shrugging, putting it to one side, bringing it up again, never quite able to leave it alone.
>
> (pp. 150–51)

Student P, who is aiming towards Grade 5, begins like this:

1 Clumsy expression: 'persuaded' would be better.

Chrissie and Rodney have talked Kathy, Ruth and Tommy into going with them to Norfolk for the day. This is because they want to ask the three Hailsham students what they have to do to get their donations put off so that they can have a few years together because they love each other.

In this passage the five of them are sitting at a table in a cafe and they all seem quite a bit scared. Kathy thinks that Chrissie and Rodney have rehearsed for months what they want to say and imagines the conversations they've had 'leading up to this moment.' Ruth, typically, pretends to be better informed than, and therefore superior to, everyone else.

2 Shows a clear understanding of Ruth's character.

Kathy reports the reactions of the others and notices 'a strange atmosphere' and a 'tingle.' Ishiguro puts Kathy's comments in a short paragraph on their own, which makes them more dramatic. Like Tommy, she is puzzled, because when they were at their boarding school nobody ever said anything about deferrals.

3 Pleasing use of quotations integrated into sentences.

4 Shows awareness of Ishiguro's method but requires further explanation.

Student Q, who is likely to achieve a Grade 8, begins like this:

**1** A clear opening statement that immediately takes us out of the passage and into a response to the novel as a whole.

**3** Uses appropriate terminology for AO2.

> Chrissie and Rodney are older than Kathy, Ruth and Tommy. They have had longer to ponder their future in the knowledge that, unless there's some action they can take, they will be separated, become carers and quite soon donors who die at fourth donation. Ishiguro doesn't spell out their fear of the future but it's very clearly present in the tension he creates as Chrissie earnestly starts to speak. The 'strange atmosphere' and 'tingle' that go round the group add to this. So does Chrissie's nervous, hesitant diction: 'really properly in love, then the people at Hailsham, they sorted it out for you'. You can almost hear the verbal gulp between the words 'Hailsham' and 'they'. They are desperate for a future and for hope, which is why they are for a moment 'hypnotised' when they see a look of 'authority' on Ruth's face.

**2** Displays understanding of Ishiguro's technique.

**4** Chooses quotations carefully and embeds them well.

Student P continues:

> In a way, all five students are showing that their afraid of the future. None of them really wants to be a donor and this deferrals rumour seems, for a few seconds, to bring a bit of hope. Soon after this passage, though, Chrissie — very disappointed — has to accept that the Hailsham students can't help her.
>
> Fear of the future, which Ishiguro makes so clear in this passage, is a major theme in Never Let Me Go. Ishiguro hints at it when he makes Kathy and her friends so frightened of the woods surrounding Hailsham. Those woods are a symbol of the dark future that is set out for them. They will become donors, suffer and die — although the students don't think about it openly while they're at school. That's because Miss Emily believes they should be protected from the truth.
>
> Another occasion when we see fear of the future coming through is much later in the novel, when

**1** Beware of spelling errors; this should be 'they're'.

**2** Shows clear awareness of the plot and structure of the novel.

**3** Focus on the question emerging and some comment on Ishiguro's style, which could be further developed.

**4** Uses appropriate terminology.

95

Ruth tells Kathy bitterly that if you're not a donor you can't possibly know what it's really like to be lying 'on that table, trying to cling onto life.' Then there are Tommy's rages both at school and at the end of the novel after he and Kathy visit Miss Emily. They show that Tommy is frightened of, and angry about, everything that is going to happen to him.

**5** Appropriate quotation is effectively used.

Student Q continues:

Kathy and Tommy, meanwhile, are puzzled because they heard of nothing like this at Hailsham. Ruth hides her own reaction because she's about to pretend that she knows something the others don't – her usual strategy for coping with fear and uncertainty. She does the same thing back at school when she pretends that her pencil case was a special gift from Miss Geraldine rather than a routine purchase from one of the Sales, and later when she is very dismissive of Tommy's Gallery theory.

**1** Excellent way of connecting the issues in the passage with the novel as a whole, as the question directs.

Kathy, with accurate insight – quite unusual for a narrator who normally suppresses her own fears behind euphemistic evasion and unconvincing self-delusion – immediately imagines the private conversations between Chrissie and Rodney that must have led up to this moment. They have, she realises, been 'probing and prodding this subject between them' for a long time and been 'bringing it up, at first very tentatively, shrugging, putting it to one side, bringing it up again, never quite able to leave it alone.' This is the behaviour of frightened people and it's only because Kathy is deeply frightened herself that she recognises so readily exactly what is going on, and has gone on before. This is, she realises, actually why they have come to Norfolk for the day. The search for Ruth's 'possible' is just an excuse, as Kathy half-suspected earlier, commenting that she thought Chrissie was 'up to something' when she first mentioned Ruth's possible, because it was all too neat.

**2** Offers perceptive comments on Kathy as narrator.

**3** Insightful comment linked to title.

**4** Reveals detailed knowledge of the novel.

As so often in *Never Let Me Go*, Ishiguro's presentation of fear of the future is made all the more powerful and disturbing by being hinted at rather than stated overtly. The same thing happens when Miss Lucy makes her well-meant but – according to Miss Emily much later – misguided revelations to the students because she wants them to know and accept what will happen to them without protecting them from the truth by obfuscation. In fact the students deal with it by continuing to hope and look forward in denial of the truth, because Ishiguro seems to be suggesting that that is how many human beings deal with the prospect of death. We've all, to a greater or lesser extent, been 'told and not told', like the Hailsham students.

**5** Explains effect of Ishiguro's style.

**6** Further exploration of Ishiguro's underlying purpose.

Student P concludes:

The moment in the café, though, seems to be the first time Kathy, Ruth and Tommy have heard deferrals openly discussed. There's so much they don't talk about – they use euphemisms and at school and the Cottages they are mostly cut off from the outside world – that this seems quite a shock. It is as if a taboo has been broken because an unmentionable subject comes up.

**1** Appropriate use of terminology.

We later hear that Chrissie and Rodney have been separated and have 'completed', which means they have been killed by having their organs removed, in different parts of the country. Their fears have come true, as they do for every student in the novel. Ruth and Tommy are both dead before the end of the novel and Kathy is about to end her long service as a carer, meaning she will start donating in a few months.

**2** Discussion of what happens beyond the passage, as the question requires.

Ishiguro shows us Kathy's own fear in the words he writes for her. She never mentions what's about to happen to her. Her fear is presented by Ishiguro by her use of very controlled language, including many

**3** Effect of Ishiguro's language choices is clearly explained (AO2), although it would be better to put this earlier in the essay rather than in the conclusion.

monosyllables ('Ruth had on one of her faces when you couldn't tell what was going on'), which makes it seem as if she is talking all on one note. As a result of Ishiguro's style, Kathy never seems relaxed because she's hiding her true feelings and fear of the future.

This essay is generally coherent and engaged and achieves a Grade 5. The response occasionally loses focus but mostly shows a clear understanding of the novel.

Student Q concludes:

Similarly, Ishiguro makes sure the reader notices that once students have moved on from the Cottages, they are rarely mentioned. These former students will have gone on to be carers, and eventually donors who die, but the students, by mutual unspoken consent, talk very little about them or where they are now. No one at the Cottages wants to think about the future and what lies immediately ahead, so they half-pretend that those who have moved on never existed. It's a way of dealing with their fear of the future – simply to carry on as if it isn't there. And it's a common tactic in real life too. Ishiguro wants us to reflect on the inevitability of our own mortality and how we deal with it.

**1** Sustained and convincing response to the text.

It is only at the very end of the novel, after Kathy and Tommy have visited Miss Emily and Madame, that they are finally forced to confront their fears and the reality that faces them because, at last, there is no alternative. Ishiguro presents Tommy dealing with this by succumbing to one final and terrible outburst of uncontrolled anger – presumably as a form of release – on the way back to his recovery centre from Littlehampton, by discussing with Kathy his fears that the fourth donation won't actually be final and then by sending her away because he doesn't want her with him

**2** Ability to speculate critically on possible meaning.

3 Displays an apt use of integrated quotation.

during 'this last bit'. Kathy, in contrast, stricken with grief and loss, deals with it by simply crying a little and turning from the spot in Norfolk that symbolises everything she has lost and the life she will soon lose, and going to 'wherever it was I was supposed to be', her fear held down as usual.

4 Offers an elegant ending, picking up the very end of the novel and Kathy's suppressed fears.

Student Q meets most of the criteria for Grade 8. The response is sustained and convincing and integrates the text effectively. Coverage of AO2 is a little less strong.

As your examination will be 'closed book', you might find it helpful to memorise some quotations to use in support of your points. This section provides quotations relating to the key moments in the action of the novel, the main characters and the themes, as well as an indication of why each quotation is important.

## Top ten moments

**1** 'Then he began to scream and shout, a nonsensical jumble of swear words and insults.' (p. 9)

- The first description of Tommy having a tantrum. This will be counterpointed by his tantrum towards the end of the novel.

**2** '...what I was doing was swaying about slowly in time to the song, holding an imaginary baby to my breast.' (p. 71)

- Kathy plays her Judy Bridgewater tape and, brought up in full knowledge of her own infertility, imagines that she has a baby of her own in her arms. Madame passes by and disconcerts Kathy by weeping. This incident is important in that it reveals the very natural emotional reactions of clones and confirms their humanity, as well as then setting up an enigma regarding Madame's reaction.

**3** '...as he threw up his arm, he knocked my hand aside and hit the side of my face.' (p. 11)

- During one of Tommy's dramatic rages – which merely amuse the other Hailsham students – the young Kathy approaches Tommy in an attempt to comfort him. He accidentally hits her and this effectively marks the beginning of their friendship. His hurting her while loving her anticipates the way he finally banishes her (p. 277) as he approaches fourth donation.

**4** Miss Lucy: 'Your lives are set out for you. You'll become adults, then before you're old, before you're even middle-aged, you'll start to donate your vital organs.' (p. 80)

- Miss Lucy believes that every student should understand what the future holds and not be protected from the truth. This is the first time in the novel that Ishiguro sets out the future clearly – because it's Miss Lucy's voice we hear for a moment, rather than Kathy's.

'I checked each model's face before moving on.' (p. 132)

**5**

- Frightened of her own sexuality, which she doesn't understand, Kathy becomes convinced that she must have been modelled from a pornographic model or someone similar. Although not clearly explained at this point in the novel, it does hint to the reader that Kathy too feels the need to search for her identity.

Chrissie: '…the people who run Hailsham, they sorted it out for you. They sorted it out so you could have a few years together before you began your donations.' (p. 151)

**6**

- The real purpose of the trip to Norfolk is for Chrissie to ask the Hailsham students how she and Rodney can get a deferral (p. 153). This is the first time that the idea of deferrals is raised. It's quite a dramatic incident, with a 'tingle' in the 'strange' atmosphere, and is significant because the idea of a deferral recurs later in connection to Kathy and Tommy.

'Tommy seemed to become aware for the first time just how frail she was.' (p. 218)

**7**

- Tommy and Kathy, on the way to visit the boat with Ruth, become aware of her physical deterioration. This foreshadows the terrible future that awaits them all and adds a note of urgency to what follows.

Ruth: 'You and Tommy, you've got to try and get a deferral.' (p. 228)

**8**

- Ruth is remorseful over her past conduct and urges Kathy and Tommy to visit Madame with a view to deferring their donations. This is a crucial plot development since it raises hopes and leads to the climax of the novel when these desperate hopes are ultimately dashed.

'When we had proper sex and we were really happy about it, even then, this same nagging feeling would always be there.' (p. 235)

**9**

- Having been friends all their lives, once Kathy becomes Tommy's carer the situation changes between them and they become a couple (p. 234). She talks only of 'having sex', but it is clear that she loves him but isn't admitting it to herself or the reader. The shadow of the future, however, still hangs over them.

**10** Miss Emily: 'There's no truth in the rumour. I'm sorry. I truly am.' (p. 253)
- Miss Emily bluntly tells Kathy and Tommy that there is nothing whatever to be done about the future that faces them as donors (pp. 251–64). It is the final dashing of all hope. It leads to Tommy's tantrum on the way home, his sending away of Kathy, and to Kathy's desperate – but still controlled – despair at the end of the novel.

# Top ten character quotations

**1** 'It's like with my memories of Tommy and of Ruth. Once I'm able to have a quieter life, in whichever centre they send me to, I'll have Hailsham with me, safely in my head, and that'll be something no one can take away.' (p. 281)
- Kathy reflects at the end of the novel that memories are very important because, unlike your hopes or even your organs, they cannot be removed. It shows her still suppressing her fears and emotions, despite what she's now facing.

**2** '...and although the tears rolled down my face, I wasn't sobbing or out of control. I just waited a bit, then turned back to the car to drive off to wherever it was I was supposed to be.' (p. 282)
- This statement at the very end of the novel shows Kathy suppressing everything she really feels – the disappointment and loss she has endured – and calmly accepting, or convincing herself that she does, that her fate is entirely in the hands of others.

**3** 'All the guardedness, all the suspicions between me and Ruth evaporated and we seemed to remember everything we'd once meant to each other.' (p. 230)
- Ruth and Kathy, who is now her carer, have been to see Tommy and have become much easier with each other. This comment gives us a glimpse of how close Kathy recalls having felt to Ruth in the past. It illustrates the tensions in their friendship.

**4** Tommy to Kathy: 'I think Miss Lucy was right. Not Miss Emily.' (p. 168)
- Devastated by the news that there is no chance of a deferral, Tommy wishes he'd always known the truth about his future. This was what Miss Lucy advocated in opposition to Miss Emily, who believed it is right to protect students and give them a childhood and education.

'Maybe come the end of the year when I'm no longer a carer I'll be able to listen to it [the tape] more.' (p. 64)

**5**

- Ishiguro shows us Kathy warmly convincing herself that she is positively looking forward to the next stage of her life, which will mean first donation and the first step towards certain death. It's fairly typical of her positive denial of the truth.

Ruth to Kathy: 'How you've got guts and how you always do what you say you're going to do. He told me once that if he was in a corner he'd rather have you backing him than any of the boys.' (p. 102)

**6**

- Ruth tells Kathy what Tommy has said about her (Kathy). This is a useful take on Kathy's character because, although it's coming third-hand, it isn't, for once, Kathy's own voice. We see her fleetingly from someone else's point of view, although Ishiguro also wants us to notice that he has made Kathy repeat it – an indication that she is flattered by these words, perhaps.

Ruth to Kathy: 'So that's it, that's what's upsetting poor little Kathy. Ruth isn't paying enough attention to her. Ruth's got big new friends and baby sister isn't getting played with so often…' (p. 122)

**7**

- Ruth's unpleasant sneering tone, in a conversation not long after their arrival at the Cottages, shows how brittle and insecure she is. It is also evidence that she has been coping with her situation by pretending and manipulating others ever since she played imaginary horses with Kathy when they were young children at Hailsham.

'And Ruth had been at her best: encouraging, funny, tactful, wise.' (p. 126)

**8**

- Still at the Cottages, this is Ishiguro revealing through Kathy the other side of Ruth's multi-faceted character. This is the charismatic friend whom Kathy feels able to trust and confide in over bedtime drinks. Her trust later proves misplaced because Ruth doesn't keep Kathy's sexual anxiety to herself, and her suggestion that Kathy's urges might stem from 'the different food we're eating here' shows how laughably ignorant she is.

'It wasn't long after that I made my decision, and once I'd made it, I never wavered.' (p. 199)

**9**

- Ishiguro has Kathy, disconcerted by Ruth's assertion that Tommy will never be sexually interested in a girl who has slept with others, finally deciding to leave the Cottages – after which she sees neither Ruth nor Tommy for several years. Much later, when she is close to death (p. 228), Ruth apologises for deliberately keeping Kathy and Tommy apart – another example of her manipulativeness – and encourages them to get together as a couple.

## 10
'...if...we did find ourselves going for a deferral, it might prove a real drawback if we'd never had sex.' (p. 234)

- This is Kathy, carefully presented by Ishiguro, trying to rationalise to both herself and the reader why she finally initiates sex with Tommy. The real subtextual reason, of course, is that she is in love with him and this is the natural thing to do, but Kathy is a habitual suppressor of her true feelings and emotions.

# Top ten theme quotations

## 1
Fear: 'Maybe all of us at Hailsham had little secrets like that – little private nooks created out of thin air where we could go off alone with our fears and longings.' (p. 73)

- Kathy explains how the students coped with their fears. Such 'places' help them to deal with fear of the future and the need to suppress natural longings, such as wanting to grow up and have a family.

## 2
Humanity: 'Here was the world, requiring students to donate. While that remained the case, there would always be a barrier against seeing you as properly human.' (p. 258)

- Miss Emily sums up the 'outside world', the public attitude to the donation programme. If people think it's right to harvest organs from a living body compulsorily, then they are not going to allow themselves to see the donor as a full human being like them. (This is not unlike the attitude to slavery in the past.)

## 3
Loss/death: 'Poor creatures. I wish I could help you. But now you're by yourselves.' (p. 267)

- Madame struggles to express her helpless anguish when she bids farewell to Kathy and Tommy at the end of the novel, knowing that they have no future other than to be surgically harvested for their organs.

Humanity: 'We took away your art because we thought it would reveal your souls. Or to put it more finely, we did it to *prove you had souls at all*.' (p. 255)

**4**

- Miss Emily explains the crux of Hailsham thinking. All human beings, even clones, have souls. Their art proves this. As things turned out, though, she and Madame failed to convince anyone. The death of the students is inevitable.

Fear: 'It wasn't him on that table, trying to cling onto life.' (p. 222)

**5**

- Ruth is angered by Tommy's assumption that Rodney would have known how it felt for his partner Chrissie when she 'completed' at second donation. This quotation gives an unusually graphic glimpse of the physical reality of donation and provides a brief insight into the fears of any donor.

Fear/death: 'Because it doesn't really matter how well your guardians prepare you: all the talks, videos, discussions, warnings, none of that can really bring it home.' (p. 36)

**6**

- Ishiguro presents Kathy reflecting on the contrast between the superficially idyllic life students enjoy at Hailsham and the horror of the future that awaits them.

Fear: '…but they seemed to us oddly crooked, like when you draw a picture of a friend, and it's almost right but not quite, and the face on the sheet gives you the creeps.' (p. 116)

**7**

- On arrival at the Cottages Kathy is still aware of the menace that surrounds them. As at Hailsham there are hills in the distance, symbolising the dark future that awaits all the students.

Death: '…and I wouldn't mind at all if that's where I ended up.' (p. 17)

**8**

- Kathy describes Ruth's recovery centre at Dover and pretends to herself and to the reader that she'd be happy to be a patient there – hiding her real feelings both from the reader and from herself, as she usually does.

Education: '…you've been told and not told…' (p. 79)

**9**

- Miss Lucy's summary of the Hailsham policy of trying to give students short-term fulfilled lives without ever spelling out the future honestly. No one actually denies the students the truth, but it is presented in such a way that they don't grasp the full horror because, as Miss Emily explains on page 263, the students would otherwise have said 'it was all pointless'.

## 10

Fear/friendship: '...fearful of the world around us, and – no matter how much we despised ourselves – unable quite to let each other go.' (p. 118)

- This thematic reference to the title of the novel relates both to the theme of fear of the future and to that of friendship. There is quite tight bonding among Hailsham students and they are drawn closer together, united by shared happy memories as the reality of the terrifying future closes in. That is why, years after they leave Hailsham, Ishiguro takes Kathy back to both Ruth and Tommy and is why she mentions each encounter with a Hailsham student as she goes about her work as a carer.

## Other fiction by Kazuo Ishiguro

- *A Pale View of Hills* (1982)
- *An Artist of the Floating World* (1986)
- *The Remains of the Day* (1989)
- *The Unconsoled* (1995)
- *When We Were Orphans* (2000)
- *Nocturnes: Five Stories of Music and Nightfall* (2009)
- *The Buried Giant* (2015)

All published by Faber and Faber.

Of these, *The Remains of the Day* is probably the most readily comparable with *Never Let Me Go*. Narrated by a 1930s butler looking back, it details his suppressed relationship with the housekeeper, against a background of the narrator's master having secret meetings with senior Germans.

## Other fiction featuring involuntary organ donation

- *Spares* by Michael Marshall Smith (HarperCollins, 1996) – presents a man who works in a donation-collection centre, who then realises that the clones providing the organs are human.
- *Under the Skin* by Michael Faber (Canongate, 2000) – a sinister story of a woman (or is she?) whose job is to pick up hitchhikers on a lonely road in Scotland and deliver them to an organ-harvesting farm.
- *My Sister's Keeper* by Jodi Picoult (Simon & Schuster, 2004) – about a 13-year-old American girl whose parents expect her to donate a kidney to her sister who is dying of leukaemia.

## Relevant science fiction

- *Frankenstein* by Mary Shelley (1818) – describes the creation of an artificial man in a laboratory by Dr Frankenstein. Once the monster is free to roam, the question is: how human is it/he?
- *The Handmaid's Tale* by Margaret Atwood (Bloomsbury, 1995) – about a world in which almost all women are infertile. So the handful who are not – the handmaids – are forced to act as surrogates through an elaborately contrived way of living.

## Other resources

- 'A sinister harvest' by Theo Tait – review of *Never Let Me Go* published in *The Daily Telegraph*, 13 March 2005.

- 'Clone alone' by M John Harrison – review of *Never Let Me Go* published in the *Guardian*, 25 February 2005.
- 'Artist of a floating world' by Andrew Barrow – review of *Never Let Me Go*, published in *The Independent*, 25 February 2005.
- An internet search for 'Never Let Me Go Kazuo Ishiguro reviews' will produce reviews published in other newspapers and magazines.
- Ishiguro was interviewed for the *Guardian* when *Never Let Me Go* was published: www.theguardian.com/books/2005/feb/20/fiction. kazuoishiguro

Answers to the 'Review your learning' sections.

## Context (p. 17)

1   After World War II and during the 1950s.
2   Cancer, motor neurone disease, heart disease.
3   An organism artificially created from genetically modified cells, rather than through sexual reproduction and a mixture of genes from two parents.
4   Judy Bridgewater's music is included to show the significance of popular music to young people in adolescence.
5   It was reviewed at length and in depth in a number of national newspapers when first published.
6   The acceptance of death and its unexpected nature.
7   The medical and scientific discoveries were made so fast and held out such hope for sick people that there was no time to think about ethics properly. This can happen in real life too.

## Plot and structure (p. 32)

1   As a reward for being an exceptionally good carer.
2   Miss Geraldine.
3   *Songs After Dark* by Judy Bridgewater.
4   The Cottages.
5   He thinks he'll need it to show that he's fully human.
6   Littlehampton.
7   It was probably stolen by Ruth. She shares a bedroom with Kathy and its disappearance is sudden and absolute. Ruth is over-zealous in helping Kathy search for it and more interested than is reasonable when Kathy eventually acquires a replacement.
8   They want to get the three Hailsham students right away so that they can ask them about deferrals. There is an assumption that, because Ruth, Tommy and Kathy are from Hailsham, they are an elite and will know things that students from elsewhere do not.
9   The Morningdale scandal turns public opinion against establishments like Hailsham and results in their closure.
10  He is frightened of the future and fears that because Kathy isn't yet a donor she cannot fully understand. He also feels that if there is no future for their love then they have to part.

### Characterisation (p. 48)

1 She refers to herself as Kathy H.
2 The boys play a trick on him and the girls laugh at him.
3 She can be overbearing.
4 She apologises and tries to make amends; we see her increasing frailty and her considerable suffering as she dies.
5 They introduce the possibility of deferrals, an idea that later becomes very important to Tommy and Kathy.
6 Through the forming of Ruth's 'secret guard'.
7 Miss Lucy. She believes it is wrong for the students to be raised in ignorance of their fate.
8 The writer uses it to suggest that she is desperate for love and attention.
9 He has discovered that the deferral rumour is just a myth. All hope is gone.
10 She is meekly accepting her fate.

### Themes (p. 61)

1 An idea that is threaded through the novel in different forms. Ishiguro uses them to weave together his ideas about respect for humanity, growing up, relationships, death and more into the story that he is telling.
2 Any three of: humanity, death, fear, education, friendship, love, loss.
3 Any two of: Chrissie and Rodney's loss of each other; Tommy and Kathy's loss of each other; Tommy's and Ruth's loss of life; loss of Hailsham; loss of Kathy's tape.
4 She and others like her are frightened of their strangeness, presumably because they are artificially created and unnatural.
5 Kathy when she is speaking to Miss Emily on page 254.

### Language, style and analysis (p. 73)

1 England in the late 1990s.
2 Ishiguro intends her narrative to sound like a chatty, oral diary rather than a formal account of her life.
3 Kathy never encounters traffic; clones passively accept their fate instead of running away; students' acquisition of spending money; the whole system would realistically be unaffordable.
4 By including Kathy's description of the horrific rumours relating to the woods – the boy found tied to a tree with hands and feet removed, the ghost of a girl desperately trying to get in.

5   She doesn't reveal her innermost fears. Instead she keeps telling us that she's looking forward to a rest when she stops being a carer. She is devastated to lose Tommy but doesn't spell out her grief. Almost everything Ishiguro gives her to write/say indicates suppression and denial.

6   Ishiguro has her describe seemingly trivial incidents (such as the guarding of Miss Geraldine or the loss of her tape) in exaggerated detail. She repeats herself, like a nervous tic, e.g. 'I don't know how it was where you were.'

7   Loneliness and inevitable death. Like the students, the boat is destined to be broken up and destroyed by forces it cannot control or change.

8   The fact that Miss Emily sets store by her possessions. The significance of the sale of it is that she has financial difficulties.

## Tackling the exams (p. 81)

1   For AQA: Paper 2 Modern texts and poetry.
    For WJEC Eduqas: Component 2 Post-1914 prose/drama.
    For OCR: Paper 1 Modern and literary heritage texts.

2   No.

3   Yes for AQA.
    No for WJEC Eduqas and OCR.

4   For AQA: approximately 45 minutes.
    For WJEC Eduqas: about 50 minutes.
    For OCR: 1 hour and 15 minutes.

5   Embed short, relevant quotations carefully to support your points, making sure the grammar of your sentence flows properly round the quotation. You can also refer closely to incidents in the novel without quoting directly.

6   Yes for AQA and WJEC Eduqas.
    No for OCR.

7   Plan your essay answer to make sure that it makes several strong points in response to the question and that it reads like a coherent, well-constructed piece of writing. Planning will also help you organise your ideas.

8   Read your work through. If you can improve it by the deletion or addition of a word or phrase, do so. Check the clarity of your work carefully, especially the spelling and punctuation.

## Assessment Objectives and skills (p. 85)

1   Your ability to read, understand and respond to texts, using textual references and quotations to support your ideas.

2    Ishiguro's writing techniques and the effects created by them.

3    It refers to the social, cultural and historical context of *Never Let Me Go*.

4    Spelling, Punctuation and Grammar.

5    AQA: AO1, AO2, AO3, AO4.
     WJEC Eduqas: AO1, AO2, AO4.
     OCR: AO1, AO2, AO3.